NOURISH
YOUR BRAIN

COOKBOOK

NOURISH YOUR BRAIN

COOKBOOK

Discover how to keep your brain healthy
with 60 delicious recipes

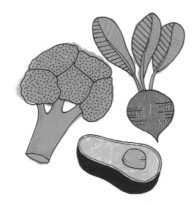

RIKA K. KECK

ACN, CMTA, FDN-P

CICO BOOKS

LONDON NEW YORK

For Dan,
and for Mom, Dad, Natti, and Poots

Published in 2017 by CICO Books
An imprint of Ryland Peters & Small Ltd
20–21 Jockey's Fields   341 E 116th St
London WC1R 4BW   New York, NY 10029

www.rylandpeters.com

10 9 8 7 6 5 4 3 2 1

Editor: Rosie Fairhead
Designer: Louise Leffler
Illustrator: Kate Sutton

Commissioning editor: Kristine Pidkameny
Senior editor: Carmel Edmonds
Art director: Sally Powell
Production controller: David Hearn
Publishing manager: Penny Craig
Publisher: Cindy Richards

Neither the author nor the publisher can be held
responsible for any claim arising out of the general
information and recipes provided in this book.
Individuals are solely responsible for their nutritional
choices. If you have food sensitivities or allergies,
or are taking any medications, discuss your
dietary choices with a health professional
or doctor. This book is intended for informational
purposes only.

A CIP catalog record for this book is available from the
Library of Congress and the British Library.

ISBN: 978-1-78249-495-9

Printed in China

CONTENTS

INTRODUCTION

I was thrilled to be asked to collaborate on this book. Taking care of my brain health feels personal, because after passing out twice from accidental blows to the head when I was young, and surviving a terrifying car wreck that left me with a head and neck injury, I know what it's like not being able to stand for more than an hour before the headaches start. The accident was the beginning of debilitating migraines with nausea, excruciating pain, and fatigue. It played a big part in why I am a nutrition and health practitioner today, because I wanted to find answers and natural solutions, and not rely on medication for the rest of my life. Dietary changes greatly decreased my migraines, and so I want to share that information with you.

In addition to my own journey, today I am bearing witness to clients who are living with the challenges associated with Parkinson's disease, Alzheimer's, Lyme disease, memory loss, concussion, anxiety and psychiatric disorders, learning disabilities, and migraines.

The following matter a great deal when it comes to brain health:

- Foods that trigger headaches
- Environmental toxins that contribute to brain inflammation, including mercury, aluminum, and lead
- Infections, such as Lyme disease, toxic mold, bacteria, and viruses
- Post-traumatic stress disorder
- Traumatic brain injuries, including concussions
- Menstrual-related migraines
- Gluten, histamine, and oxalate-related headaches
- Mast cell disorder
- Genetic predispositions that make it difficult to clear toxins from the body
- Chemical exposures
- The interconnection between the gut microbiome and the brain

The food we eat today contains fewer nutrients than that grown a century ago. The soil is depleted of many minerals and vitamins by commercial agricultural farming practices, so plants and trees are more susceptible to pests and fail to thrive. A landmark study involving 43 different fruits and vegetables showed decreased nutrients such as vitamins C, E, calcium, iron, zinc, magnesium, potassium, and riboflavin (vitamin B2) (see www.scientificamerican.com/article/soil-depletion-and-nutrition-loss). Fertilizers and excessive use of poisonous pesticides and herbicides also contribute to nutrient deficiencies, obesity, and hormonal disruption in humans—and to poor brain health, too. As memory and cognitive function diminishes, so does our quality of life.

Opposite, clockwise from top left: Gut–Brain Juggernaut Purple Sauerkraut with Dulse and Caraway Seeds (page 124); Summer Salad with Healthy Fats and Crunchy Seeds (page 74); Low-sugar Chocolate Mousse (page 147); Green-a-colada to Protect Your Brain (page 128).

We are constantly being marketed convenience and "fake" foods (and medications that create additional nutrient deficiencies in the brain and body). Mass-produced food is loaded with refined sugar, empty calories, colorants, and additives, so I urge individuals to buy organic and to support local farmers, or join an organic produce-buying club.

The growth of farmers' markets and increasing awareness among consumers of the need for organic, pasture-raised, or sustainably harvested foods is encouraging. Additional global pushback including resistance to unhealthy fast foods, growth hormones in commercial animal foods and fish, and GMO foods is heartening. We are empowered by being (mostly) able to choose what ends up in our smoothie, in our lunchbox, on our dinner plate.

Each individual is unique in his or her nutritional needs. Our ancestry, the climate we live in, and our individual metabolic needs determine whether our body prefers a lighter Mediterranean-style cuisine or a more protein-based nutritional strategy. In these times of increased food sensitivities, it is important to choose foods that make you feel alive and well. The recipes provided in this fabulous book offer many menu options that you can begin to integrate into your life.

The busier and more stressed we are, the more we need to create a space of calm and peace where we can nourish the body, mind, and soul. This happens at the table with a delicious meal in an intimate setting or with fun company. It is time for us to return to the source of health, beginning with whole foods, preferably cooked at home. Explore, experiment, and be creative in your meal-planning, put technology aside, and become present to the essence of life.

With all this in mind, I invite you to share with me carefully chosen recipes that provide the nutrients our brain needs to function well. They all have one thread in common: They help to nourish and heal the brain. We have only one brain, so we must love it and nurture it, daily.

Welcome! Now it is time to join hands around the table and cheerfully say:
"Guten Appetit, wir haben uns alle lieb!"
(Good appetite, we love one another)

Rika

Cooking Notes

- Both American (US cups plus imperial) and British (metric) measurements and ingredients are included in these recipes for your convenience. However, it is important to work with one set of measurements and not alternate between the two within a recipe.

- All spoon measurements are level unless otherwise specified.

- Ovens should be preheated to the specified temperature. Recipes in this book were tested using a regular oven. If using a fan-assisted/convection oven, follow the manufacturer's instructions for adjusting temperatures.

- All eggs are large (US) or medium (UK), unless otherwise specified. It is recommended that free-range, organic eggs are used whenever possible. Recipes containing raw or partially cooked egg, or raw fish or shellfish, should not be served to the very young, very old, anyone with a compromised immune system or pregnant women.

- When a recipe calls for the grated zest of citrus fruit, buy unwaxed fruit and wash well before use. If you can only find treated fruit, scrub well in warm soapy water and rinse before using.

- If you are allergic to gluten, dairy, eggs, nuts, corn, or soy, please check all labeling carefully before buying ingredients for use in these recipes.

- Oats are inherently gluten free, but because they are mostly processed in facilities that also process glutenous grains, most brands are cross-contaminated with gluten and therefore not suitable for coeliacs. If you need to avoid gluten entirely, look for oats that are labeled "gluten-free."

- When a recipe calls for frozen fruit there is no need to defrost the fruit before using.

- There are many different brands of protein powders available and each have varying portion recommendations based on their specific blend of proteins. Standard scoop sizes vary (3/4–3 oz./20–60 g) but most brands usually provide a 1-portion scoop or list the portion size on the packaging. Always refer to the packet instructions when following these recipes.

- Sterilize preserving jars before use. Wash them in hot, soapy water and rinse in boiling water. Place in a large pan and cover with hot water. With the lid on, bring the water to the boil and continue boiling for 15 minutes. Turn off the heat, then leave the jars in the hot water until just before they are to be filled. Invert them onto clean paper towels (kitchen paper) to dry. Sterilize the lids for 5 minutes, by boiling, or according to the manufacturer's instructions. Jars should be filled and sealed while still hot.

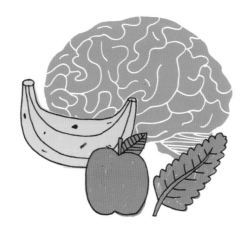

PART 1

THE BASICS FOR A HEALTHY BRAIN

The Brain:
Powering Your Day

While we go about our busy lives juggling life and work commitments throughout the day, we hardly think about the most important organ in our head—our brain. Different areas of our brain allow us to hear sounds, smell aromas, think and speak freely, move our limbs, breathe, memorize experiences, interpret information from the outside world, and learn new things that are useful in our lives.

Think about it: If you stub your little toe, it hurts. Your brain knows that too. If you are dehydrated on a hot day, you could end up with a headache—yes, your brain needs water too, and it begins to shrink when you are dehydrated. If you get excited because you walked into a surprise birthday party and your heart pumps with excitement, your brain is charged up, too, with excitable brain chemicals and adrenaline. All are simple examples of how the brain is implicated in every situation.

Our skull, which comprises 28 bones, houses the brain and protects it from physical trauma such as blows to the head or concussion. The head weighs about 8–12 lb. (3.6–5.4 kg) and the brain roughly 3 lb. (1.4 kg). The brain, which is composed mostly of fat (especially cholesterol), contains various components, all with their own function, with billions of nerves that communicate constantly via electrical signals.

The blood–brain barrier acts like a border-control agent by separating the brain from the bloodstream. It keeps toxins out, but allows essential nutrients to enter—after all, the brain must be fed too. If the integrity of this membrane is compromised, we end up with a "leaky brain" that toxins and infections can harm. This is part of an inflammatory process associated with various degenerative neurological diseases, toxicity, and premature aging. The good news is that through what you eat, you can directly lower inflammation (see page 23) in the brain, while also allowing the brain to heal.

The brain is a complex organ that enables us to sense danger, or to relax when we feel safe and secure in our surroundings. It is very sensitive and responds to any perceived stress, whether positive or negative. Such responses can include giddiness when you get your dream job, or when you worry about money. A primal "fight or flight" survival response is the result, and it takes tremendous energy for the body to respond, at the expense of hormones and the immune system. Technological advances have escalated the pace of life and stress levels, and for many today there is simply not enough sleep, rest, or play.

Top Eight Basic Brain Facts

1 The complex brain is comprised of three sections, of which the largest is the cerebrum. It controls functions such as vision, hearing, touch interpretation, and learning.

2 Underneath the cerebrum is the cerebellum, which controls functions such as movement, posture, and balance.

3 Lastly, the brainstem functions as a conductor between the other parts of the brain and the spinal cord, which runs down inside the spine. Automatic functions that we are not aware of are governed by this area, including breathing, digestion, body-temperature regulation, and sleep cycles.

4 The brain is divided into right and left hemispheres, which are interconnected in their function. The left is in charge of writing, speech, logical thinking, and understanding, while the right is in charge of creativity, artistic skill, musical inclination, and spatial ability.

5 Many nerves are also involved with the brain. Our central nervous system (CNS) consists of the brain and the spinal cord, and the peripheral nervous system (PNS) branches out from the CNS.

6 Glands include the hypothalamus, pituitary, pineal, and thalamus glands, and affect hormonal balance, immune function, cognition, and fertility.

7 The brain has an intricate blood supply. Weakness in the blood vessels are associated with bleeding in the brain (aneurism).

8 Our emotional consciousness is contained in the limbic center of the brain.

Physical trauma, infections such as strep (streptococcal infections) or Lyme disease, and accumulated environmental toxins such as mercury and aluminum harm the brain. Food sensitivities also inflame the brain. Over many months and years, chronic inflammation in the brain can result in:

- Mental health problems
- Declining mood and behavior
- Sleep disorders
- Ongoing pain
- Memory loss
- Nerve damage
- Cognitive dysfunction
- Vision, balance, speech, and hearing disturbances
- Tangles and plaque formation (including beta-amyloid plaques, which can also be considered as protective or compensatory, and a pathological mechanism. Research is ongoing)

The Spirulina and Matcha Brain-fitness Bites on page 149 help to improve mental clarity and lower stress levels.

Food for Thought

How we manage stress, beginning with a healthy eating, exercise, and sleep strategy, will have great impact on the long-term wellness of our brain. Consider, for example, that a deficiency of vitamin B12 is associated with dementia and tingling sensations in feet and fingers. Every day, every meal, it matters what and when we eat, as our blood-sugar balance and brain energy depend on it. A nutrient-deprived brain ages faster.

Even at night, our brain does not rest when we do. While we sleep, the brain ensures that we breathe and maintain steady blood sugar, and that our heart keeps beating. It also processes and stores information gathered during the busy day, reinforcing our memory. Not only that, but housecleaning in the brain also occurs at night. While we sleep, the brain shrinks slightly, and the lymphatic fluid can sweep out accumulated toxins that contribute to inflammation and premature aging.

It is particularly important to nourish a developing brain in a young child, and an aging brain in the later stages of life, when often more nutrients are needed than are supplied in the daily diet. Sadly, foods today contain much lower levels of vitamins and minerals than did the foods our grandparents ate. Skipping meals creates an energy crisis, depriving the brain of the energy it needs if we are to think clearly.

At any age, the brain needs stimulation to create new nerve pathways (neuroplasticity) to improve mental adaptation and behavioral flexibility. Learning, cognitive behavior therapy, crossword puzzles, meditation, and mindfulness practices all have the potential to rewire the brain for the better. Daily movement is also needed to maintain the flow of life—oxygen and blood. To perform at the highest level, while maintaining a zestful life with fun and joy, requires a well-nourished brain.

The Gut-Brain Connection

A "Double-Header"—Our Gut-Brain Connection

You know what it feels like when you smell freshly baked cookies and your mouth waters. You also know what it is like when you have a gut feeling about a situation, or when you feel sick to your stomach when you are very upset. You also know how emotionally satisfied you can feel after you have enjoyed a delicious meal with loved ones.

Our brain and gut are closely interconnected in terms of our senses, biological functions, emotions, and moods. Every piece of food we consume and every stressful thought we have affects our brain directly, in both gut and head. Both "brains" need to be nourished if we wish to perform well, maintain mental energy, and stay emotionally balanced.

Unhealthy processed or junk foods irritate the stomach—and they will irritate the brain, too. They contribute to inflammation in the gut and brain, and over time that can contribute to many illnesses, including autoimmune diseases, developmental problems in children, painful joints, cognitive difficulties, and degenerative neurological diseases in adults.

Time for a little anatomy: Our two "brains" are closely connected by a complex nervous system that relies heavily on the vagus nerve. This large nerve is like the captain of the ship, conducting information back and forth from the brain to all the organs and glands that are involved with our digestion, breathing, and heart function. It is also known as the gut–brain axis.

The digestive tract is like a rubber tube that runs from the mouth down to the anus. Millions of nerves are embedded in its walls, and that is why we can feel pain and other symptoms if we have trouble digesting certain foods. This network of nerves is the enteric nervous system, and it is also known as the "second brain." The gut tube has a mucosal lining of gut-associated lymphoid tissue that forms a large part of our immune system. Its role is to provide a protective boundary between the outside world and our inside body. It is often said that all disease begins in the gut.

When foods move from the mouth through the digestive tract, many different hormones, nerves, and digestive enzymes are called to action by the gut–brain in our innards. Digestion requires a lot of energy; after all, it is the biggest driver of our metabolic fire. Too much stress in daily life, and a lack of nutrients such as zinc, affects the body's ability to release stomach acid and enzymes that are essential for healthy digestion and the absorption of nutrients. Both too much and too little stomach acid is a problem.

Any undigested food that putrefies and ferments in the stomach invites harmful microbes and yeasts to feast on it. At the same time, you may be noticing digestive symptoms such as acid reflux, gastric inflammation, bloating, excessive gas, or constipation, while your mind is experiencing ADHD (attention deficit hyperactivity disorder), anxiety, brain fog, and funky moods. You might also experience itchy skin, sleep difficulties, or tightness in the chest (do consult a cardiologist if you have this last symptom, to rule out cardiovascular problems). In addition, any difficulties with elimination or excessive bowel activity are an indicator of digestive troubles that can originate higher up.

Inflammation is the immune system's biochemical response to stress, brain trauma, infection, surgery, or physical injury. Acute inflammation is a stressful event, and it uses a lot of our nutrient reserves and hormones during this time, but it must be seen in a positive light. It is the body's way of healing itself, of trying to get us back to health. In this all-out healing effort the immune system releases chemicals called cytokines to heal a leaky gut lining, or overcome an infection such as a virus or food poisoning.

Concussion, symptoms related to autism, post-traumatic stress disorder (PTSD), or early symptoms of Parkinson's disease or dementia are brain-based phenomena, but they can cause great digestive troubles, microbial imbalances, and a leaky gut. The developing brain is especially sensitive to physical trauma, toxins, and infection. Contrary to popular belief, neurodegenerative disease happens in young people, too. Epilepsy, diabetes with autonomic neuropathy, multiple sclerosis (MS), and lupus can occur in adolescence, as can autoimmune encephalitis, Lyme disease, symptoms of mercury exposure, and amyotrophic lateral sclerosis (also known as motor neuron disease). All these affect the nervous system in the brain, and as a result can induce digestive dysfunction along the esophagus and the entire digestive tract.

Let's Talk about Microbes

Today, we have a lot more scientific information, especially after the Human Microbiome Project (HMP) in the United States, that shows how a diverse gut flora plays an important part in our resilience (physical, mental, and emotional), our outlook on life, and our ability to maintain a rational mindset. The project was sponsored by the National Institute of Health to explore the function and diversity of microorganisms in the human gut that are associated with health and disease.

In fact, our microbial makeup and diversity play a greater role in our wellness than does our genetic makeup. Think of your gut flora as an internal soil and garden that you carry around with you wherever you go. This ecology becomes a lifelong template that promotes or decreases our physical health and mental wellbeing. It needs tending, just like the vegetable patch in a backyard. What we eat affects our microbes and our moods directly. Fiber in fruit and vegetables is known to be a prebiotic that optimizes the balance of our bowel flora and absorption of nutrients. It provides the "feed" for the various probiotic strains that have a direct connection with our psychology and our ability to think clearly from the moment we get up in the morning.

Prebiotic vs. Probiotic

Think of prebiotics as a fertilizer that consists of specialized plant fibers. Insoluble fiber from fruit, vegetables, and grains is fermented and converted into short-chain fatty acids called butyrate, which becomes a source of food for various strains of health-supporting bacteria in the colon. Butyrate is often deficient in many chronic illnesses and autoimmune diseases, including colitis and irritable bowel syndrome (IBS). Prebiotics feed the good microbes in our gut. Examples in food include the inulin in bananas, fiber in garlic, leeks, onions, avocados, legumes, coconut flakes, and guar gum (found in many processed foods). Additional prebiotic supplementation includes fructooligosaccharides (FOS), psyllium husk, and acacia.

The Very Pink Yogurt Smoothie and Coconut Kefir Smoothie on page 137 include both prebiotics and probiotics for a healthier gut.

Probiotics are live bacteria that are part of the human body's microbiome. They eat prebiotics, and so the more fiber-rich foods we incorporate into our diet, the happier the health-supporting microbes are in our gut. They are the good cops that keep out, crowd out, and combat the baddies. Well-known examples are species of *Lactobacillus*, including *L. bifidus* and *L. acidophilus*, and a healthy yeast called *Saccharomyces boulardii*. Probiotics occur naturally in cultured and fermented foods such as kefir, yogurt, sauerkraut, tempeh, miso, and pickles. (It is also possible to supplement your diet with and soil- and spore-based probiotics. These beneficial microbes add to the diversity within an individual's gut flora. I find them helpful in a variety of digestive ailments in rotation with other probiotic strains, but recommend consulting with a health practitioner to discuss which probiotic choice is best for you.)

Artificial sweeteners, processed foods with excess sugar, and rancid fats do not contain the fiber and nutrients that are needed for a healthy bowel flora, and tap water containing fluoride and chlorine kills health-supporting microbes. The overgrowth of harmful organisms, parasites, bacteria, and yeasts, such as candida in the gut, will affect our mental wellbeing. Harmful yeasts and microbes release poisons into our body that contribute to brain fog, anxiety, depression, poor mood and concentration, lack of mental energy, and trouble sleeping.

Dark, leafy greens, multicolored vegetables, fermented foods, and healthy fats from nuts, seeds, pasture-raised animals, and fish, all help our body to get rid of the toxins that we are exposed to daily. Fermented foods and drinks such as sauerkraut, kimchee, kombucha, and kefir encourage health-supporting bacteria and yeasts in our gut, but are not in the mainstream diet. We need them, however, since they play an important part in maintaining our mood and energy.

Top Five Facts
about the Microbial Gut–Brain Connection

1   **Synthesis of vitamins and minerals.** The microbes in our gut (known as the microbiata) are like busy construction workers on a work site. They help to break down foods into bioavailable vitamins such as the vitamin B complex, which nourishes the nerves in the brain.

2   **Childhood development.** A diverse microbial blueprint has an enormous effect on babies' development, learning capacity, ability to fight childhood infections, and food sensitivities. The unique gut flora is established initially by vaginal delivery, breastfeeding, and parental contact. If a C-section is required, or breastfeeding is not possible, infant probiotics can be worth considering.

3   **Detoxification.** Getting rid of toxins is a vital part of keeping the brain well and alert at any age. Microbes in the gut help our body to metabolize toxins so that they can be eliminated, stopping them from building up inside our body and poisoning our brain.

4   **"The Defenders."** Microbes in our gut are gatekeepers; they can fend off harmful pathogens such as the parasites that can enter your body when you eat your favorite sushi. Think of the microbes as your internal defense system (in conjunction with hydrochloric acid in your stomach).

5   **"The Forgotten Organ."** A diverse community of microbes in the gut—the microbiome or "the forgotten organ"—helps to modulate stress and increases the production of serotonin for mood and melatonin for sleep. Lack of diversity can lead to food cravings, weight gain, and depression. (In studies, autistic children have been shown to have less diverse gut bacteria than the general group.) In conventional medicine, certain antidepressant medications are prescribed for patients with IBS, since psychological stress can alter the perception of pain and the muscle activity in the gut associated with IBS. This shows how our emotions and psychological outlook are closely connected with the nerves in our gut via the gut–brain axis. This interconnection was explored as early as the 1920s by Dr. Élie Metchnikoff, who said that he encountered no cases of psychiatric illness where digestive function was not compromised.

Feed Your Gut—and Your Brain!

Fermented foods These make the nutrients in food easier to absorb and provide a variety of health-supporting probiotics. Try kefir in a smoothie, sauerkraut with your grilled chicken breast, or pickles as a twist to your summer salad.

Fruity fruit and varied veggies The enzymes, minerals, and vitamins found in raw foods, salads, and smoothies help to heal tissues, and are part of various biochemical processes that affect our energy and our ability to handle the stress of daily life. Vitamins A, K, and C in these foods help to heal a leaky gut. The more colors on your plate at each meal, the better. Every day, create a kaleidoscope of hues to provide the brain and body with a variety of phytonutrients:

Blueberries contain flavonoids, which help to reduce the risk of cancer and are great for the health of the brain and the heart.

- Tannins are the water-soluble phenols found in grape skins, cocoa, tea, sage, cranberries, and red wine. They have astringent properties, and their health benefits include the inhibition of plaque formation on teeth, the healing of wounds, and the alleviation of gastritis and diarrhea.
- Flavonoids are phytonutrients that have anti-cancer, heart-healthy, and brain-healthy properties, while also improving memory and microcirculation in the brain. They are found in plant-based foods and determine the color of the vegetable or fruit: the darker the color, the better, as in blueberries, purple grapes, blackberries, parsley, black beans, capers, and green tea.

- Organosulfur compounds are essential minerals needed for the detoxification pathways that play an important role in our ability to eliminate environmental toxins, chemical estrogens in plastics, and infections. A lack of these may increase our risk of cancer of the reproductive organs. Sulfur-containing foods from the animal and plant kingdom include eggs (especially the white), meat, and vegetables such as broccoli, cabbage, bok choy (pak choi), turnips, onions, garlic, and leeks.
- Resveratrol is a potent antioxidant and anti-inflammatory found in certain fruits, red wine, and cocoa. It increases microcirculation in the brain and heart, and is a memory, vision, and immune modulator. Resveratrol can cross the blood–brain barrier. (Incidentally, Japanese knotweed, a great source of resveratrol, is used in botanical treatments for Lyme disease.)

Eat whole The skin of organic fruit also has health benefits, but this is not widely known. Grate some fresh orange peel over your salad or breakfast bowl for detox agents in the quercetin and limonene family. If you are going to eat fruit skins it is doubly important that you go organic, since most pesticides are contained within the skin—and do wash it well.

Healing herbs We infuse herbal medicine into our home-cooked meals when we add rosemary, thyme, oregano, sage, bay leaf, savory, marjoram, basil, parsley, or cilantro (coriander). Herbs will lift the taste of any hot dish, or chop some fresh herbs as a decorative anti-inflammatory addition to your summer salad.

Spice it up Cumin, cloves, cayenne pepper, paprika, cinnamon, and more are staples in a spice rack for a healthy kitchen. Spices have great nutritional and medicinal value and improve our cognition and memory. Curcumin, the active component of golden turmeric, has been shown to encourage the growth of new neurons while also altering degenerative processes in the brain. That is exciting news! Curcumin has powerful anti-aging, anti-inflammatory, and anti-cancer properties, and has been used in

traditional medicine for many centuries. Today many use a daily turmeric supplement against pain and inflammation, although not everyone tolerates turmeric. (Before using any supplementation do check with your doctor if you are on blood-thinning medication, or have gallbladder trouble or diabetes.)

Enjoy a cup of tea Choose any herbal tea or elixir and add a sprig of lemongrass or rosemary to connect with your sense of wellness. It has been established that green tea contains the phytonutrient EGCG (epigallocatechin-3-gallate), which helps the body to get rid of toxins, has anti-cancer properties, and is anti-inflammatory. All that in one cup of tea!

Daily detox Garlic, which contains the active phytonutrient allicin, has the potential to lower blood pressure while providing sulfur for detox. Foods such as broccoli, cabbages, radishes, and dark, leafy greens are also dense in phytonutrients. They contain a compound called sulforaphane, which promotes the elimination of harmful chemicals, chemical estrogens in plastics, and environmental toxins. The more toxins we can get rid of, the more we will protect our brain in the long term.

Opposite: Herbs are anti-inflammatory as well as a great way to add flavor.
Above and above right: Fennel and artichokes are full of fiber, which is essential for the optimal performance of the gut.
Below right: The Chicken Tikka Masala on page 90 is filled with spices that improve our memory and boost our immune system.

Fabulous fiber High-fiber foods such as bananas, yams, leeks, avocado, cassava, artichoke, asparagus, fennel, okra, chickpeas, and couscous are all food sources for microbes. They get their energy by fermenting the fiber in these whole foods. It's important to feed our friendly microbes, so that they can feed our brain.

Broth (stock) The elixir for "leaky gut syndrome" can be found in chicken (especially the gelatin-rich chicken feet and also pigs' feet), beef, lamb, fish, and their bones. The amino acids, trace minerals, gelatin, and collagen they contain improve digestion, help to heal mucosal linings in the brain and gut, and provide overall nourishment.

Supplementation The use of probiotics is helpful, and various options are available.

Leaky Gut/Leaky Brain:
The Autoimmune Disease Connection

If the mucosal barrier in the gut is breached or becomes porous in places, intestinal semi-permeability arises, commonly known as leaky gut. This breach triggers an inflammatory process that can have far-reaching effects if the body is not able to heal it within a few days. Pesticides, especially glyphosate, in commercial foods cause or contribute to a leaky gut, which is associated with sustained inflammation. All can leave you constantly fatigued and weakened with multiple food sensitivities and trouble with learning, memory, and cognitive function.

If a leaky gut continues unchecked for months or even years, food particles, allergens, toxins, and infectious agents can gain entry into the body. This wreaks havoc, as the immune system becomes hyper-vigilant and cannot distinguish self from non-self. This is the basis of most autoimmune diseases. Healthy tissues in the body will be attacked, and this can affect the brain, thyroid, pancreas, colon, joints, skin, and more. We can experience headaches, pain, insomnia, and anxiety as our stress meter is dialed up.

Acute brain trauma (such as a concussion when playing sport, a traumatic brain injury or TBI in a car accident, or the injuries many soldiers suffer abroad with roadside bombs) will induce a leaky gut within four hours. Changes occur in the mucosal lining of the gut, and this opens up tight junctions, allowing larger molecules of food to pass through into the bloodstream. This also happens in the brain—in an innate inflammatory response, the blood–brain barrier becomes "leaky" as the immune system tries to gain access through it in order to repair damage to neurons in the brain. (The immune system is not supposed to be active in the brain, but it will be in the case of infection, trauma, plaque build-up, gluten sensitivity, and autoimmune disease.)

Toxic ingredients and preservatives such as formaldehyde, mercury, and aluminum in vaccinations, environmental toxins such as lead in water or daily makeup, and gluten in food can all breach the blood–brain barrier, and brain inflammation results as the immune system becomes irritated. A leaky brain is associated with epilepsy, Alzheimer's, MS, autism-related symptoms, and autoimmune encephalitis. A toxic and inflamed brain can result in seizures, learning problems, cognitive difficulties, and behavioral, psychiatric, and neurological problems. This is not considered in conventional psychiatry, gastroenterology, or pediatrics.

Autoimmune disease can be triggered by a variety of factors, including:

- Processed ingredients, such as gluten, trans fats, food coloring, chemicals, and flavorings
- Environmental toxins, including phthalates, PCBs (polychlorinated biphenyls), arsenic, and aluminum
- Exposure to mold in water-damaged buildings
- Pesticides, insecticides, and herbicides
- Antibiotics in medical care and in conventional foods
- Excessive alcohol consumption
- Infections such as strep or Lyme disease, or physical trauma such as a blow to the head
- Trauma or emotional, sexual, or psychological abuse of any kind
- Surgery

Top 15 Foods, Herbs, and Spices for Lowering Inflammation

- papaya
- blueberries
- ginger
- avocados
- rosemary
- bone broth (stock)
- turmeric
- celery
- dark leafy greens
- beets (beetroot) and tops
- fatty wild-caught fish
- garlic
- chamomile
- cod-liver oil
- okra

Chronic inflammation associated with a leaky gut and leaky brain plays a role in many neurological diseases, chronic pain, migraines, and psychiatric conditions. Consider it as an ongoing low-grade irritant to the body that diminishes our resilience and makes us age faster on the outside and the inside. Even though we might not be aware of it, the immune system is irritated by the accumulation of environmental toxins, lack of sleep, medications, emotional, financial, or work stress, personal relationship troubles, and more. All contribute to low-grade sustained inflammation that adversely affects blood sugar balance, energy production, cognition, mood, and memory, and it depletes our nutrient reserves, thyroid function, and reproductive hormones.

The healthy proteins, fats, and carbohydrates in the delicious recipes in this book take all the above into account. Vitamins in whole foods help nerve function, heal the stomach lining, and lower inflammation in the brain. Minerals in animal and plant foods enable communication between brain cells. Enzymes found in raw foods, salads, and smoothies help to heal tissues and are part of various biochemical processes that affect our energy and mood.

Friend or Foe Food List

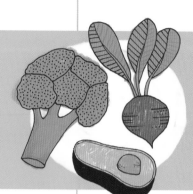

Friend

Multicolored organic vegetables and fruit that provide an array of vitamins and minerals needed for the healthy function of the brain. These include carrots, broccoli, celery, avocado, salads, dark leafy greens, beets (beetroot), onions, garlic, blueberries, pineapple, and grapes.

Free-range poultry, pasture-raised animals, organ meats, and by-products (such as eggs, butter, chicken fat). Include homemade broth (stock) and gelatin as bioavailable protein sources for brain and mood health.

Nuts and seeds, ideally soaked, drained, and dried. These provide a wide array of omega-3 and unrefined omega-6 oils that support healthy brain membranes and lower overall inflammation. Brazil nuts, walnuts, almonds, pecans, pistachios, macadamias, and hazelnuts are fine choices.

"Healthy brain" fats and oils, including cold-pressed olive oil, organic butter, ghee, coconut oil, lard, evening primrose oil, palm oil (from sustainable sources), and unrefined safflower, sunflower, walnut, and avocado oils.

Naturally occurring sugars in fruit, raw honey and maple syrup (preferably local), and molasses (stevia is acceptable).

Foe

Commercially processed foods with a long shelf life, excessive refined sugars, and sodium, plus fortification with synthetic vitamins that are not bioavailable for brain nutrition.

Avoid all factory-farmed animal proteins, processed breakfast and luncheon meats, and commercial poultry.

Rancid processed nuts with excessive sodium, often stored in moldy conditions that contribute to mold toxicity symptoms, including brain fog. Peanuts (actually a legume) and peanut butter are best avoided for this reason. Cashew nuts have been associated with hives and dermatitis. With a nut or tree nut allergy, do carry an Epi-pen™ to guard against anaphylaxis with accidental exposure.

Excessive fats, and all fast and deep-fried foods. Especially avoid partially hydrogenated vegetable fats (called trans fats), vegetable shortening in packaged baked goods, margarine, and cookies; all these inflame the brain and are implicated in heart disease and nerve cell death associated with neurological diseases.

Artificial sweeteners of any kind are known for their neurotoxic effect: they kill brain cells and induce hyper-excitable behavior and attention deficit disorders.

Sometimes it's difficult to know which foods to choose or to avoid. This chart will help you seek out those which are friendly toward our gut—and those that are not so friendly. (This chart is for general information only. All food allergies and food sensitivities must be respected.)

Friend	*Foe*
Home-cooked oatmeal (porridge) or grains, preferably stoneground, rich in fiber and B vitamins. Steel-cut oats or barley are favorites, but also investigate buckwheat groats, quinoa, millet, and amaranth. Chia, coconut flakes, and hemp seeds can be mixed with nuts and fruit.	Processed cereals from refined grains (GMO crops in the USA) that are low in fiber with the chemical BHT (butylated hydroxytoluene) and added colors, preservatives, and additives that irritate the brain. These non-foods are sprayed with synthetic vitamins.
Purified/filtered/spring water, ideally in glass bottles. Clean, mineral-rich water flushes out toxins from the brain.	Sodas, diet drinks, and synthetic flavored water are toxic to the brain, and can cause anxiety, migraines, and headaches.
Home-squeezed fruit and vegetable juices contain natural fiber that prevents a spike in blood sugar. Choose just one fruit serving if you juice, such as a cup of mixed berries or one banana, and add a source of protein and fat to complement it.	Processed concentrated fruit juices, even if organic, spike blood sugar and induce an exaggerated insulin response that increases inflammation, reduces cognitive flexibility, and increases weight gain.
Slow-cooking: baked, crockpot, roasted, sautéed, low-heat grilling, steamed food preparation.	Cooking at high temperatures is harmful. Any browning or blackening of foods when grilling increases inflammation and damages our body. High temperatures destroy vital nutrients, especially vitamin B6.
Preferably choose cold-water fish that lower inflammation. These include anchovies, cod, halibut, wild salmon, herring, and sardines, all of which contain healthy omega-3 fats. (Smaller fish are less contaminated with mercury.)	Tuna, king mackerel, and swordfish that contain high levels of mercury. Commercially farmed fish is contaminated with antibiotics, growth hormones, preservatives, and commercial dyes.

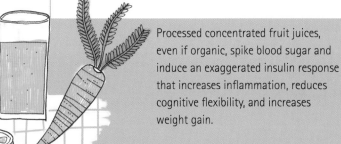

Foods that Promote Energy, Stable Moods, and Focus

You Think What You Eat!

What we eat and when we eat directly affects how well our brain functions—and that is empowering to know. All day long our brain needs a steady stream of energy from food for optimal cognition, memory, attention, happy thoughts, and stable mood. It can use glucose from carbohydrates, such as grains, vegetables, and fruits, or amino acids from various proteins, such as cheese, meats, or eggs, for energy, but it prefers various fats as a long-lasting source of fuel. The recipes in this book emphasize the various healthy fats our brain needs for daily energy, and the proteins we need for good moods.

Pregnant and nursing women, and individuals on medications should consult a health-care professional before drinking herbal teas. Respect food sensitivities.

No Sugar Coating Here

Scientific evidence shows that eating too many sugary foods contributes to an accumulation of harmful molecules, called advanced glycation end products (AGEs). These promote harmful free-radical damage from toxic molecules—think of it as internal rusting. Over many years, they contribute to low-grade brain inflammation that is associated with adult neurodegenerative diseases such as dementia, MS, Parkinson's disease, and Alzheimer's.

Junky, sugar-loaded, and commercially processed foods (I call them "dead foods") will not nourish our brain. Food and drinks containing a lot of sugar spike our blood sugar and provide a quick burst of energy that makes us feel wired. This is followed by the release of insulin—because too high a level of blood sugar is toxic to the brain—and then we can experience low blood sugar, also known as hypoglycemia. Now we feel tired and jittery, in a cranky mood, and wanting more sugary treats. Fluctuations in blood sugar place tremendous stress on the brain and

on our hormonal resources, and encourage carb addictions, overeating, anger, and aggressive behavior. Balancing the blood sugar must be the top priority on any path toward wellness.

Foods that are high in sugar make us forgetful, depressed, and wired—and increase unwanted belly fat, too. Too much sugar in the diet contributes to insulin resistance associated with obesity, type 2 diabetes, and inflammation of the brain. (There is even a type of Alzheimer's disease associated with insulin resistance, called type 3 diabetes.)

Artificial sweeteners are poisonous to the nerves in our brain and must be avoided at all costs. Like lead, arsenic, and fluoride in water, or thiomersal in vaccinations, artificial sweeteners are also known as neurotoxins that are linked with mental retardation, behavior problems, seizures, neurodegenerative diseases, and schizophrenia. Besides artificial sweeteners, it is also best to avoid chemical sugar

Top 20 (Organic) Foods for Energy, Mood, and Focus

- dark leafy vegetables, such as spinach* and kale
- purple grapes
- multicolored berries
- avocados*
- coconut oil
- free-range egg yolks*
- extra-virgin olive oil
- wild salmon (smoked, cooked, or canned)*
- rosemary
- turmeric
- gingko tea
- green tea extract
- brahmi tea
- grapeseed oil
- walnuts*
- cod-liver oil
- butter*
- dark chocolate*
- navy (haricot) beans and other foods rich in choline (see below)
- pasture-raised meat

* If you find these starred foods do not improve your energy, mood, and focus, you may be suffering from a sensitivity to them—see page 35.

substitutes or sugar alcohols with names that end in -ol, such as maltitol and sorbitol. These can irritate the brain and the digestive tract by inducing gas, bloating, stomach cramping, and (for some) a laxative effect.

Agave nectar from the Mexican blue agave plant is very popular as an alternative to natural sugar. However, most agave products sold in mainstream grocery stores are highly refined and contain high levels of pesticide residue and processed fructose syrup. It is best to check the source and ingredients of the product you wish to use.

The good news is that there are many healthy options for adding a little sweetness to your day. A serving of mixed berries, pear, banana, and cherries makes a colorful dessert plate that is naturally sweet. A Very Pink Yogurt Smoothie (see page 137) will satisfy any sweet craving. On a cold winter day, steamed and puréed yams provide a delicious side dish for your roast turkey. Raw honey, rapadura, pure maple syrup, and blackstrap molasses can be used instead of refined sugar in traditional baking recipes. Stevia, a natural herbal sweetener, is now a favorite for many (but do avoid it if you have an allergy to ragweed).

Yogurt is a fantastic source of protein, and you can add berries to it for a little healthy sweetness, just as in the Very Berry Brainy Brekkie on page 58.

Pack a Powerful Punch with Protein

For a productive and high-performing day, include a good source of protein in your breakfast. A lack of protein in the diet affects our blood-sugar balance, mood, and concentration. If you have a smaller appetite in the morning, you might prefer oatmeal (porridge), a bowl of yogurt, or a smoothie. If you have a large appetite and respond well to a hearty breakfast, enjoy an omelet or add avocado and protein powder to your smoothie.

Amino acids from proteins are building blocks for brain chemicals called neurotransmitters. It is only in this small form that they can be absorbed. There are 22 different amino acids, including:

- Lysine
- Histidine
- Methionine
- Tryptophan
- Phenylalanine
- Glycine
- Tyrosine
- Threonine

Amino acids matter because they form enzymes that are involved in every biochemical process in the body. They affect our moods and our ability to focus and think clearly. They also affect our appetite, cravings, weight management, ability to fight infections, detox-ability, reproduction, sleep patterns, and ability to heal. Our body can produce certain amino acids, but we must get some essential amino acids from foods in our daily diet. Neurotransmitters are produced in the brain, but new research shows that the production of neurotransmitters involving behavior and mood is closely linked to the microbiota of the host. It has also been shown in studies that antibiotic drugs reduce the production of one of these neurotransmitters, serotonin, by affecting the serotonin-producing microbes in the gut. Are mental-health troubles in fact related more to the intestinal flora? Science will tell. This also matters in respect of the newly emerging histamine-related sickness and mast cell disorders where, among other complex factors, excessive levels of histamine are implicated.

A vegetarian or vegan diet can insidiously induce deficiencies in fat-soluble vitamin A, B12, zinc, choline (a macronutrient that is needed for brain and nerve function), cholesterol, and amino acids. This can contribute to depressed moods as well as affecting other functions, such as bone health challenges, muscle wasting, and infertility. It is particularly important for those who follow these diets to create a good mix of protein by combining different protein groups in each meal. It is worth considering supplementation with minerals, vitamin B12, and fat soluble vitamins A, D, and K.

Soy is a popular source of protein in purely plant-based diets. However, in traditional cuisines, soy was used as a condiment and only in a fermented form to make nutrients bioavailable. Examples of organic fermented soy include natto, tempeh, and miso, and these should be eaten with seaweed on the side. The seaweed provides iodine that our thyroid requires for optimal function and it offsets the thyroid-inhibiting enzymes associated with soy. Today, popular soy-imitation foods (faux franks, veggie burgers, chicken-free chicken patties, imitation bacon-bits, soy protein isolate protein powder, and soy milk) are used as a protein replacement at meal time. These are processed foods that are high in sodium, gluten, and MSG. They also contain lignins and other enzyme inhibitors that disrupt thyroid function and block zinc, magnesium, and vitamin B12 absorption.

Soy-containing foods are a far cry from the traditional fermented and nutritious soy in the Asian cuisine, yet they are pervasive in the food chain today, especially GMO soybean oil. It is worth noting that soy is among the top five food sensitivities.

Soy infant formula is another great concern due to the high levels of phytoestrogens in soy that cause hormonal disruption in the young. Excessive soy consumption is also contributing to early breast development and menses in girls. The consumption of soy can have a feminizing effect on boys and men, as it lowers testosterone and can affect fertility. This has been associated with hypogonadism (testosterone deficiency) and "man boobs." With prevalent estrogen-dominant concerns today in teenagers and adults (men and women), and association with reproductive cancers, it is prudent not to consider soy as your major protein choice if you opt for a plant-based diet. Instead choose from a wide variety of legumes, nuts, seeds, hemp, spirulina, oils, and more to complement your food plate.

The Omega-3 Filled Smoked Salmon with Lentils, Onions, and Carrots on page 77 has more than enough protein for a superactive day.

Although some people still think egg yolks are "bad," they are in fact a healthy source of cholesterol.

The Cholesterol Conundrum

Since the 1950s, we have been told that eating saturated fat and cholesterol-rich foods is unhealthy and contributes particularly to heart disease. This was based on flawed studies. Animal fats in foods were said to cause heart disease and cholesterol problems. This was promoted by the vegetable oil industry and conventional medical community, which had strong ties to pharmaceutical industries. Harmful partially hydrogenated processed vegetable oils (including corn, canola, sunflower, cottonseed, and vegetable), margarine and other butter substitutes, and vegetable shortening for baked goods became staples in the food supply.

In traditional cultures, foods containing cholesterol-rich ingredients, including butter, pasture-raised meat, raw milk, and organ meat, were prized. The fats they contained enabled people to survive famine, because in a state of starvation, the brain turns fat into an energy source known as ketones. Our bodies still work in this primal manner, unless stress levels are too high and our body is not able to burn fat efficiently. In contrast to sugary carbohydrates, healthy fats such as coconut oil and egg yolks provide long-lasting brainpower, improved focus and concentration, and a sense of satiety, while curbing carb addictions.

Why does cholesterol matter?

- It is an important component of breast milk, and is critical for a baby's brain development and intelligence.
- It maintains the structure of cells so that they do not collapse.
- It is needed for the conversion of vitamin D, which plays many important roles in our health and longevity.
- It is vital for learning and memory, especially in the young and old.
- It is essential for the formation of bile and the absorption of fatty acids.
- It is important for fertility and libido. Cholesterol is the building material for sex hormones including estrogen, progesterone, and testosterone.
- It is the base material for our natural cortisone.
- If we do not get enough cholesterol from our diet, the body can make it, but this innate ability declines with age and the use of medication.

Thankfully, there is increasing awareness that saturated fat and cholesterol are not the villains in the food supply. With current dietary trends including the Paleo Diet, the Ketogenic Diet, and Whole30®, we are reintegrating traditional fats from responsibly farmed animals into our dietary vocabulary. Gone are the egg-white omelets, margarine, and other artificial butter substitutes; instead butter, duck fat, coconut oil, and lard are slowly making a comeback on the food plate.

Important Fats and Oils that Nourish the Brain

Saturated Fats

- More stable at higher temperatures when cooking than unrefined and monounsaturated oils.
- Found in animal foods, organ meats, broth (stock) from marrowbones, butter, cheese, yogurt, kefir, and plant oils such as palm and coconut oil.
- Egg yolks are a mega brain food, with choline that is needed for brain health (I add two raw egg yolks—bought from a farm I know—to power up my breakfast shake).
- It is essential not to compare healthy saturated fats in pasture-raised animals with those in processed foods. Saturated fats associated with processed meats, frozen and packaged meals, and takeout foods are not healthy. These tend to have been exposed to high heat. Also, processed foods usually have added GMO vegetable oils and contain high sodium, preservatives such as lab-synthesized sodium benzoate, synthetic colorants, natural and artificial flavors, high-fructose corn syrup, and other added sugars. The cumulative effect of these factors induces free-radical damage and inflammation in the brain and body.

Monounsaturated Oils (Omega-9)

- Found in olives, olive oil, almonds, pecans, and macadamia nuts.
- In scientific studies, extra-virgin olive oil has been shown to improve memory and learning.

Polyunsaturated Fats and Oils (Two Types)

Omega-3 fatty acids are best refrigerated, as they turn rancid when exposed to heat, light, and oxygen. They are abundant in fatty wild fish, free-range eggs, nuts, and seeds. Besides their anti-inflammatory action, they affect cognition, learning and memory, and decrease pain. There are three common forms:

- EPA (eicosapentaenoic acid), such as fish oil, krill, seaweed, hemp, and flaxseed oil. These anti-inflammatory fatty acids help to lower triglycerides (fat molecules found in the blood plasma), reducing the risk of stroke; they also decrease depression, and at higher doses can help to heal a leaky and injured brain, especially in cases of acute brain trauma.
- DHA (docosahexaenoic acid), found in algae or cod-liver oil, is especially necessary in developing and aging brains. It assists with cognition, learning, and memory.
- ALA (alpha-linolenic acid) is found in plant, nuts, and seed oils or butters. It is an important part of cell membranes in the brain. It may be helpful with stroke, heart health, depression, and autoimmune conditions such as lupus and rheumatoid arthritis (research is ongoing). The body can easily absorb these healthy fats from animal-based foods. In plant-based foods, the body must work harder to convert ALA into the bioavailable form of EPA and DHA.

Omega-6 fatty acids are present as linoleic acid in plant and seed oils. If processed and refined, as in mass-produced sold products, linoleic acid is inflammatory.

- Choose unrefined oils such as evening primrose, sunflower, or hempseed. Store in a cool place.
- Omega-6 fatty acids are best in a 4:1 ratio with omega-3 fatty acids. The Standard American Diet (SAD) is abundant in refined omega-6 oils in the form of corn, soybean, safflower, cottonseed, canola, vegetable and sunflower oil, and many commercially farmed nut products. It is essential to discern unrefined omega-6 oils—for example, in dark glass bottles—from cheap processed vegetable oils in white plastic bottles.
- Commercial vegetable oils are heat-treated, partially hydrogenated to extend their shelf life, and processed with solvents and chemicals. In addition, there is inadvertent consumption of rancid fats in a box of opened crackers or chips, and trans fats in baked goods. Know your fats and oils.

Energizing Your Brain

All day we need energy—and our brain does, too. Breakfast is the most important meal (or drink) of the day; after all, it really is a call to "break" the "fast" after our sleep. But it also matters how we manage the notorious mid-afternoon slump, when there is a natural dip in cortisol, our daytime hormone. Everyone is different, but we must all fuel our brain. It is very important not to skip meals to avoid a blood-sugar crash.

"Power Up" with Breakfast

Breakfast greatly affects our blood sugar. It determines whether we will enjoy good concentration for learning or performing at work, or suffer funky moods and lack of focus. What we eat and drink within the first hour of waking matters greatly. Here are some good options:

- A bowl of creamy goat yogurt with organic blueberries (sweeten with stevia if you wish) and ground flaxseeds
- A fluffy mixed-vegetable omelet with a slice of multigrain toast, or sautéed vegetables on the side for a gluten-free option
- A bowl of yummy oatmeal (porridge)

Lunch and Munch—and Make the Vegetables Crunch!

In Mediterranean cultures, lunch is a family meal, and some people even take a siesta afterward. Taking an afternoon nap is not common anymore, but it is still important to be mindful of how we fuel our brain and maintain optimal blood-sugar levels in the afternoon. This includes taking the time to sit down, without being distracted by technological devices, and shifting our presence and gratitude to the food in front of us. Such foundational points can be most difficult in the busy lifestyle of the twenty-first century, I know, but giving the brain a time-out from multitasking is very helpful. It facilitates improved digestion and the absorption of nutrients that allow us to function at the highest level.

The Performance-boosting Breakfast Bars on page 148, made from oats, banana, and raisins, can be a quick breakfast or an afternoon snack.

The midday meal can be hearty, because our digestive power is strong—yet it is at this time that we tend to eat on the go, or perhaps even skip lunch altogether, as other commitments demand our attention. The brain becomes stressed if we do not break properly to eat, and that will affect our mood and outlook on life.
A drop in blood sugar can lead to tiredness in the afternoon; protein for lunch lifts our mood and keeps our focus sharp. You might opt for:

- A hearty bowl of beef chili or mixed vegetable soup if you live in a cold climate
- A salad filled with a colorful variety of vegetables, nuts, and goat cheese
- Delicious Sesame Chicken Wraps (see page 87)

Got that Mid-Afternoon Sinking Feeling?

The mid-afternoon slump is a complaint I hear about all the time as a health practitioner. It is then that sugary treats such as cookies or candy, coffee, cigarettes, or caffeinated sodas can be tempting, because they provide instant fuel for a tired brain. They are not good for long-term alertness, though, not to mention health, so instead, when the pangs strike mid-afternoon, try:

- A yogurt smoothie sweetened with stevia or raw honey
- Tahini, Lemon, and Parsley Dip (see page 126) or hummus, with crunchy raw vegetables
- A protein-rich Paleo Cookie or Performance-boosting Breakfast Bar (see pages 138 and 148)

Dinner

These days, dinner is often the time when the family gathers around the table, or when we share food with friends, whether it's a simple meal or a fancy multi-course menu. Whatever the case, it should always involve high-quality ingredients and rainbow-colored foods that each have their unique healing properties.

Choose fresh and seasonal vegetables for color and taste. Begin with a salad or a small bowl of soup to get the digestive juices flowing. For protein, you might choose one of the following:

- Chunks of sheep cheese with an interesting array of greens, beets (beetroot), and quinoa—a lighter option
- A grilled sea bass with dark leafy greens and sweet potatoes with parsley
- Delicious Rosemary Shish Kebabs (see page 95)
- Chicken Tikka Masala (see page 90)

Why not entertain your taste buds and stimulate visual delight, not to mention improving your gut flora, by adding a condiment of fermented vegetables (such as Purple Sauerkraut with Dulse and Caraway Seeds, page 124, or Turmeric and Chile Kimchee, page 117)? Be adventurous with your food plate.

Some people prefer to enjoy a small dinner, feeling that a heavy meal in the evening affects their sleep. Traditional Chinese medicine holds that it is best to have a large breakfast, a good lunch, and a smaller dinner, as the digestive fire is not so strong in the evening. The traditional Indian system Ayurveda suggests that it is best to eat dinner before 7 pm, so that we can digest it before going to bed. At night, while we are asleep, our brain needs a steady supply of blood sugar so that we can get a good night's sleep. It is important to note that everyone is different; if you experience hypoglycemia at night, it is a good idea to experiment to find what works best for you. Some do well with a small protein snack before bed, such as a little hard cheese and nuts, or a few tablespoons of yogurt. Others do better with a carbohydrate snack, such as unsweetened applesauce with a teaspoon of coconut oil and stevia. Pay attention to how hungry you are at night once you start eating regularly during the day. Listen to your body and see what you crave—the body does not lie.

Dessert: Yes or No?

There is a place for a little sweetness in our lives and on our food plate; after all, it has healing properties that are well described in Chinese medicine. Naturally occurring sugars provide sweetness and have toning and relaxing properties, and also enhance the function of the digestive system. Moderation is key: a little

sweetness from naturally occurring sources goes a long way. If you want to lose weight, save dessert for special occasions only. Even a coconut macaroon after a meal, or a piece of organic dark chocolate with a cup of licorice-root tea, can satisfy a craving for sweetness.

An Important Note about Sensitivities

No discussion of brain health can leave out the implication of the food sensitivities that are so prevalent today, since they greatly affect our energy, mood, and focus. There are many reasons why these occur. Common root causes include antibiotics in foods, medication, stress, and gluten, all of which contribute to a leaky gut. However, a dialed-up immune system is another factor. This can be caused by infection, environmental allergies, pesticides, pollution, heavy metals, dental work, childhood vaccinations, exposure to toxic mold, and more. One must consider the overall terrain in which food sensitivities occur, since it is rarely just about the food.

Symptoms can range from ADHD, itching, swelling, bloating, brain fog, hyper-excitability, seizures, sleepiness, painful joints, headaches, and depression, to life-threatening anaphylaxis, weight gain, and more. Food allergies and sensitivities can appear immediately, or as late as 72 hours after the consumption of a food trigger.

An underlying leaky gut makes us more susceptible to food sensitivities, all of which drive inflammation in the body and brain—it is not so much that the food is a "culprit." Gluten and dairy sensitivities are implicated in the release of chemicals that have a morphine-like effect

Having a small sweet treat, perhaps made with organic dark chocolate, with a cup of tea for dessert is a great way to satisfy a craving for sweetness.

Top 14 Food Sensitivities and Trigger Foods
That Can Induce Fatigue, Headaches, Mood Swings, and Poor Concentration

- foods containing gluten
- corn
- sugar
- soy
- foods high in histamine, including spinach, ripe bananas, avocado, and salmon
- nuts

- dairy
- foods high in oxalate, including chocolate, rhubarb, and coffee
- eggs, especially egg whites
- artificial sweeteners, which are neurotoxins
- foods containing yeast

- alcohol
- foods high in salicylate, including radishes, strawberries, and wine
- nightshades, including tomato, eggplant (aubergine), potatoes, peppers of all kinds

on the brain, inducing a "food coma" with sleepiness, learning disorders, funky moods, and brain fog. Lactose intolerance can be present from birth, or acquired later in life, when the balance of gut flora is disrupted.

Changes to your diet can be very helpful in decreasing gut and brain inflammation, which are often associated with food sensitivities. If you suffer from any inflammatory condition, cognitive problems, or mood disorders, do consider eliminating gluten to see if it alleviates or even resolves the symptoms. Similarly, eliminate dairy if you have asthma, chronic sinusitis, or ongoing respiratory problems. Why not try eliminating gluten or dairy for three weeks? Note in a food diary (see page 150) how you feel, improvements in your health, and any other changes you observe. After three weeks, have a day full of gluten-containing foods, or multiple glasses of milk, as appropriate. Track how your body responds in the next few days. Food elimination is an inexpensive and effective way of seeing if foods you consume regularly do not agree with you. Your body does not lie. As with all dietary advice in this book, do obtain medical advice from a physician before making changes.

Certain food allergies, such as those to tree nuts, can be life-threatening, so if you suffer from such allergies you must always have an epinephrine (adrenalin) injection at hand in case of accidental exposure.

Final thoughts

To get through a busy day, we all need a brain that is sharp and focused, whether as kids going to school, adults at work, or simply in order to play a fun game of chess with a friend. All day long, the ability to concentrate for a prolonged time can be a challenge, especially as life for many of us is fast-paced and involves ongoing interaction with brain-stimulating technological devices. This book contains delicious recipes that provide a large variety of nutrients and brain-supporting fats and oils. Your body needs the best if you are to enjoy a life of vitality, productivity, and joy.

Rotate Your Plate

Select the Colors of the Rainbow

Nature provides us with an abundance of fruit and vegetables that delight the eye, nose, and palate. We need to eat a variety of natural compounds known as phytonutrients, polyphenols, flavonoids, ellagic acid, and carotenoids found in plant-based foods if our mind and body are to be well. Every food contains a different array of vitamins, minerals, and fiber that interacts with our unique biochemistry.

Try the Healthy and Hearty Soup to Warm the Soul, Heart, and Brain on page 82 when the weather is colder outside.

It is important to respect the climate we live in when we make our daily food choices. In colder climates or chilly weather, choose warming oatmeal (porridge), hearty soups, stews, and curries of all kinds. In sunny and warm climates or seasons, smoothies, crisp, light salads, and chilled soups help to cool the body. Availability is another important consideration: If you live in Northern Europe, for example, where the winters are rainy and gray, you may have a more limited choice of local fresh fruit and vegetables at certain times than do those who live in sunshine-filled Florida.

Food rotation is not a novel concept, nor is the emphasis on eating seasonal and local foods. Be aware that any long-term food elimination or dietary strategy that eliminates a macronutrient (such as the vegan diet, which contains no animal proteins or fats) may cause nutrient deficiencies over time. Depending on where you live, different foods will be available to you, and by eating a kaleidoscope of local fruits, medicinal mushrooms, and seasonal vegetables, you can incorporate their innate healing properties into your body.

Foods matter on an energetic level; after all, food = energy. Every color of the rainbow connects to one of the seven energetic points in our body, known as chakras. Purple, blue, green, yellow, orange, and red are the colors associated with energetic touch points that connect with organs, glands, and psychological and emotional states. To optimize our brain health, we must nourish our emotional wellness, too.

FIRST CHAKRA (ROOT)

Emotional energy:
Safety, financial security, survival, belonging to tribe

Location: Base of spine

Corresponding foods:
Root vegetables (such as beets/beetroot), pomegranate, tomatoes, cayenne, strawberries, raspberries, red bell peppers, red apples, red cherries

SACRAL CHAKRA (CREATIVITY)

Emotional energy: Creativity, passion, sense of self; associated with urinary symptoms and back pain

Location: Lower abdomen (reproductive organs and intestines)

Corresponding foods: Pumpkin, papaya, turmeric, tangerines, carrots, apricots, corn on cob, salmon, nuts, seeds, clean drinking water, herbal tea

SEVENTH CHAKRA (CROWN)

Emotional energy:
Spirituality, self-awareness, oneness with world, truth, inner knowing, gratitude

Location: Top of head, above the head

Corresponding foods:
Mushrooms, garlic, ginger, onions, lychee, cauliflower, coconut; essential oils including sage, lavender, frankincense

Food Color Wheel

THIRD CHAKRA (SOLAR PLEXIS)

Emotional energy: Personal power, self-confidence; governs digestion

Location: Stomach area

Corresponding foods: Pineapple, mango, peaches, lemon, yellow curry, turmeric, sweet potatoes, banana, oats, beans, squash, zucchini (courgettes)

SIXTH CHAKRA
(THIRD-EYE OR BROW)

Emotional energy:
Intelligence, trust, imagination, perception, focus

Location: Between eyes on forehead (center)

Corresponding foods:
Eggplant (aubergine), purple kale, grapes, purple cabbage, carrots, potatoes, cacao

FIFTH CHAKRA (THROAT)

Emotional energy:
Communication and expression, integrity, openness, intuition; blockages affect vocal strength

Location: Throat area

Corresponding foods:
Blueberries, blackberries, stone fruits (such as olives and plums), elderberries

FOURTH CHAKRA (HEART)

Emotional energy: Love, joy, inner peace, forgiveness, grief, energy, compassion

Location: Center of chest

Corresponding foods: Green raw foods and juices, broccoli, asparagus, parsley, dandelion, chard, green bell peppers, green apples, avocado, mint, green tea

Also consider the wisdom of traditional Chinese medicine, which incorporates five tastes: bitter, sweet, sour, pungent, and hot. Such qualities are reflected in certain foods, and they enhance the way our body functions. You can harness this by adding bitter dandelions to a meal to stimulate digestion, for example, or indulging a sweet craving with a fruity shake. When we listen to our body, it will give us clues.

Let's not forget about the power of mushrooms! These saprophytic organisms are a delicious source of protein for any dish. Some can poison us—but others can help to heal us. Certain culinary mushrooms have anti-cancer, antimicrobial, and antiviral properties, and thus protect our brain from outside infections, so I would always include such medicinal mushrooms in my dietary arsenal. Let's take a look at some you can find in the store or gourmet food market:

Mushrooms have various benefits, and shiitake mushrooms such as these can help reduce the risk of cancer.

- Shiitake mushrooms have antiviral and anti-cancer effects. Do remove the stem, though.
- Cordyceps mushrooms are immune- and energy-boosters that you can add to soups or stews, or drink as tea.
- Maitake mushrooms are associated with improving blood-sugar balance and reducing blood pressure.
- Lion's mane is my favorite (perhaps because of my African roots). Besides stimulating nerve growth and helping motility in the gut (the ability to move food through the digestive tract), in a Japanese study lion's mane was shown to aid mild cognitive impairment.

The body enjoys diverse tastes, textures, and flavors, so mix up cooked and raw foods. Our body needs enzymes for many functions in the body, especially as we age. Raw vegetables and fruit are a great source of enzymes and of fiber that feeds our gut bacteria. A condiment of fermented or pickled vegetables enhances every lunch or dinner table.

Rotating foods is also an excellent way of avoiding and decreasing food sensitivities. By changing up the foods we eat, we are less likely to become sensitive to foods. And, we give the body a chance to dial down its inflammatory response if we unknowingly consume a food that it is sensitive to. If we eat the same foods daily, such as a morning corn muffin or soy protein shake, we are more susceptible to developing food sensitivities as the immune system becomes agitated. This goes hand-in-hand with inflammation. By ingesting an array of colors and a variety of foods, we encourage energy, longevity and happy moods.

Who doesn't enjoy a lunch or dinner plate filled with different colors, textures, and aromas that awaken our senses and appetite, and get our digestive juices flowing? Variety is the spice of life—and the same is true of food.

Lifestyle Matters

During our lifetime, our nutrition and lifestyle have the greatest impact on our health and longevity. The huge availability of food (and calories) in today's developed world, and our sedentary lifestyles, contributes to many degenerative and chronic diseases, including type 2 diabetes, high blood pressure, and weight gain.

We can (and should) eat organic food but that is not enough to keep us well. Sleep and exercise are fundamental—sleep to keep our brain sharp, and regular movement to maintain flexibility, strength, and stamina—yet these can present a challenge for many.

Take a look at the quiz that follows, and place a check mark next to the questions that you answer "Yes" to today:

Nutrition and Lifestyle Quiz

- Do you skip breakfast during the week because you are in a hurry to get to school or work?
- Are you addicted to caffeine in the morning and during the day, to increase your energy and focus?
- Do you drink processed orange juice every morning?
- Do you eat a bowl of conventional cereal every morning?

Why not start your day by supercharging your brainpower? Within an hour of waking up, eat a protein-dense breakfast, such as a Fruit Yogurt Brekkie, or drink a smoothie if you do not feel very hungry. Mix it up to keep it interesting! Freshly squeezed fruit with fiber (and healthy fats) prevents a spike in blood sugar. Too much caffeine will leave you feeling "wired but tired." Enjoy a cup of organic coffee or tea with breakfast, not instead of breakfast, and perhaps choose a revitalizing tonic in the afternoon. Do be aware that commercial coffee is high in pesticides, and the paper cups handed out at coffee shops are lined with chemical estrogens that leach into your hot drink. It is best to brew your own at home or at work and enjoy it in a porcelain cup, or choose a BPA-free stainless-steel cup when on the go.

- Do you go on carb binges, including eating cereal or sweets at night?

Got the late-night munchies? Manage your blood sugar by avoiding alcohol and sweet treats at night. If you have late-night cravings, learn how to tell whether you are truly hungry, or just emotionally hungry. Alcohol, TV, and empty carbs for dinner can cause this, but it can also be caused by stress. We are all different, so experiment with a combination of protein and fat or a fruit snack late at night. Cheese and other dairy treats can satisfy the brain, or try applesauce with stevia.

• **Do you eat fast food, TV dinners, frozen pizzas, and other junk food regularly?**

Conventionally processed foods, fast foods and frozen foods are loaded with excess sodium, which contributes to high blood pressure, water retention, and headaches. (Processed table salt is roughly 40 percent sodium. Sodium is also found in MSG, preservatives, and baking soda in packaged foods and baked goods.)

• **Do you add table salt to your food?**

Sea salt and Himalayan and Celtic salt contain essential trace minerals that our brain and body need. They do not contain the aluminum or the anti-clumping or bleaching agents that are used in the production of commercial table salt.

• **Do you drink tap water?**

Generally, tap water is contaminated with chlorine, fluoride, arsenic, residue from pharmaceuticals, copper from rusty pipes, and more. All are toxic to the brain, and the cumulative effect has been implicated in brain inflammation (although this is not yet accepted in conventional medicine). Our brain requires daily hydration if it is to function well. Invest in a water filter for your kitchen to ensure that you and your family are drinking clean water at home. (There are many options to suit various budgets.)

• **Do you eat lunch in a hurry at work?**
• **Do you eat lunch sitting at your desk?**
• **Do you look at a screen when you eat?**

When you have a meal or a snack, try to put the outside world on hold. We are far too busy "doing," so set boundaries and take time for yourself. It may not always be possible to find quiet surroundings, but do mentally create a calm space for yourself so that you can consume your meal. Become mindful of sitting down, noticing how you sit (slouching or with good posture, with your legs side by side, rather than crossed, so that circulation can flow). Loosen a shirt button or your necktie if you feel constrained. You can use various techniques to reduce stress while you nourish your body with nutrient-dense foods:

• Place your feet on the floor, become rooted, and connect with Mother Earth.
• Switch handheld electronic devices to silent or even airplane mode and put them to one side.
• Turn off the TV, which distracts the brain and keeps you wired in survival mode.
• Become mindful of nourishing your body, and breathe slowly to shift out of survival mode.
• Enjoy the aroma of the food you are about to eat.
• Relish the different colors of the food, which are a feast for the eyes and the stomach.
• Chew the food until it liquefies in the mouth. Chewing is the most important part of our digestion, as it initiates the release of digestive enzymes and bile needed for the absorption of foods.
• Say inner thanks—I call this expressing gratitude for the gifts of our planet.
• Become present.

• **Do you consume alcohol every day?**

Alcohol is socially acceptable and for many it is part of their lifestyle. However, it is also a brain toxin that contributes to a leaky brain and siphons vitamins A, B1, B2, B6, and C and many minerals from the body. Even though it might take the edge off a stressful day, it also contributes to weight gain, dehydration, blood-sugar fluctuations during the night, high blood pressure, headaches, increased risk of breast cancer, pancreatitis, liver dysfunction, yeast overgrowth, brain fog, and digestive tract troubles.

- Are you addicted to your electronic devices—even late at night?
- Do you have trouble falling asleep or staying asleep?
- Do you regularly get less than 8 hours' sleep because of going to bed too late?

Your brain needs rest if it is to recharge—and that is why sleep is so vital. The best sleep occurs before midnight. Exposure to blue light from technological devices and electromagnetic frequencies at night affect our ability to produce melatonin, our sleep-inducing hormone, and these are also implicated in inducing a leaky brain and attention disorders. Do eliminate all electromagnetic devices in the bedroom. They interfere with the electrical activity of your brain and affect your ability to get restorative sleep during the night. If you use your phone as an alarm clock, put it on "airplane" mode during the night. Put up blackout shades to ensure a dark room, and keep your sleeping environment cool. A sleeping mask and ear plugs can be helpful if you are trying to sleep in a noisy city.

- Is regular exercise part of your lifestyle?

Regular movement and exercise train the heart muscles so that you have more energy in your tank—and your brain becomes saturated with oxygen and your circulation improves, too. It is scientifically proven that regular exercise acts as an antidepressant and decreases pain. Climbing stairs every day at home, school, or work is a good idea; playing tennis outside in the fresh air is fun; and taking a daily walk is a gentle way to get your circulation going. Or why not join a dance class where you can learn to "move and groove"?

- Are you using organic skincare products, and going "green" at home?

Let's talk about home cleaning goods and personal care products. Go "green" and go organic. Every toxin you smell, breathe in, or apply to your skin will make its way into the brain, where it accumulates. For example, regular lipsticks or lip glosses contain detectable levels of lead, cadmium, aluminum, and other harmful metals and chemicals that girls and women unknowingly swallow and absorb every day. (This is particularly dangerous for pregnant women, because these metals are associated with neurological and cognitive problems in developing fetuses.)

Final thoughts

A busy day requires lots of stamina and brainpower. After our many daily commitments, we cherish putting our feet up in the evening. Let's face it, life is busy, and most of us are more sedentary today than ever before. Besides being attentive to what and how we eat, we must up our game when it comes to lifestyle, exercise, sleep, and stress reduction, and—very importantly—limit our exposure to ever-increasing environmental toxins and electronic devices (do not put your cell phone in a shirt or pants pocket, where it can disrupt your heart and reproductive organs.) Foundational factors such as nutrition and lifestyle affect the brain's ability to heal inflammation after injury, to think good thoughts, to retain new information, and to recall all our fond memories. We have only one brain, and it must last a lifetime.

Choose organic skincare products to avoid harmful toxins reaching the brain via the skin.

PART 2

THE RECIPES

What to Stock in Your Pantry

Life is busy, and quite often one needs to create a meal in a pinch. If you keep a basic selection of whole foods, herbs, and spices in your pantry, you will be amazed at how easy it is to create a quick meal from scratch. It can take time to build up a stock of ingredients for the pantry; some you will use frequently, such as almond butter, olive oil, or coconut oil, and others only occasionally, such as capers or fennel seeds. When it comes to your individual pantry, allow your nutritional needs and your lifestyle to guide you.

If you prefer to plan your menus ahead, write out what special ingredients you will need and take the list with you on your next shopping trip. This might be a gluten-free soy sauce, or dried green lentils that you must prepare ahead of time. Or you might prefer to "buy as you need." When pressed for prep time, you might pick up a cage-free (free-range) roast chicken as an addition to a delicious salad for dinner.

Frozen or fresh berries, dried cranberries, chia seeds, and coconut milk are terrific to have on hand for a morning smoothie or dessert delight. You will always need sea salt and flaxseed, coconut, and olive oils—and other oils, such as avocado or sesame. (It is better to buy smaller bottles of oil, so that they do not sit in your pantry for too long and turn rancid.) It is always handy to have lemons, garlic, and onions on the countertop—a ready addition to almost any meal. My refrigerator is stocked with raw butter, olives, feta cheese, goat yogurt, kimchee, mustard, and raw apple cider vinegar, while fresh arugula (rocket), bell peppers, and cucumbers are ready to go in the crisper. Marrowbones, ground lamb meat, and free-range meat are in the freezer to be called on for dinner. Frozen meat is best not left at room temperature on the countertop to thaw out, since that encourages the growth of harmful bacteria. Instead, plan ahead and thaw out foods in the refrigerator. A faster option is to use a cold-water bath: wrap the frozen food in a plastic bag, making sure it is completely sealed, and then submerge it in cold water. You will need to change the water a few times before it reaches room temperature. The time required depends on the size and type of food, so always check that it has defrosted completely before you cook it. Never run frozen meat directly under cold water as it can spread bacteria and risks food poisoning.

Here is a list of staple ingredients that are a great foundation for your brain-health pantry and will provide various meal options:

- Cooked cereals, including steel-cut oats and cream of buckwheat for porridge
- Chia seeds and dried goji berries
- Protein powder and powdered gelatin for morning shakes
- Sugars: raw honey, maple syrup, stevia, coconut sugar, rapadura
- Spices: turmeric, cayenne, cumin, cinnamon, sage, nutmeg, paprika
- Dried herbs: herbes de provence, oregano, savory, basil, sage, fennel seeds, rosemary, and marjoram
- Ready-made tomato sauce for pasta or other dishes, artichokes, ginger, pickles, yellow mustard, olives, anchovies, all in glass jars

Keep dried foods, such as rice and pulses, in your kitchen pantry.

- Dried goods, including jasmine or basmati rice and lentil or chickpea pasta
- Baking goods: gluten-free flour, arrowroot flour, almond or coconut flour, buckwheat, aluminum-free baking powder, vanilla and almond extracts, cocoa powder
- Dried pulses or legumes
- BPA-free cans of sardines and wild salmon
- Oils, including olive, coconut, and unrefined safflower oil. Also duck fat in a glass jar
- Raw apple cider vinegar, balsamic and rice vinegar
- Wakame or dulse seaweed for soups
- Nut and seed butters: organic almond butter or sunflower-seed butter (unsweetened), tahini

- For entertaining: gluten-free party crackers, rice crackers, baked chips (crisps), oatcakes
- Herbal teas, including green tea and various caffeine-free options, such as hibiscus
- Organic dark chocolate

Over time, other foods accumulate in the pantry as one becomes more adventurous. If you incorporate the brain-healthy recipes in this book into your daily menu-planning, your pantry will become a foodie's paradise.

Let us not forget the countertop, where we ripen foods in the sun. Avocados, bananas, tomatoes, and bell peppers all ripen quickly this way. Many fruit and vegetables in big grocery stores are picked when they are unripe, and thus do not have access to the full array of soil nutrients that allow them to ripen into a nutrient-rich food. Many ripen (or, in fact, rot) on their way from field to store. Try growing vegetables at home if possible, or support your local farmer or farmers' market.

With children, special celebrations, or guests, extra foods always manage to make their way into the pantry. The following list shows just how your stocks can grow:

- Cherry jam with cane sugar
- Organic chocolate spread that kids love
- Almond or rice milk, unsweetened and unflavored
- Miso paste
- Ready-made stock—this can be a "meal-saver" in a pinch
- Coconut water, for summer
- Organic tomato sauce
- Chutney to accompany any curry dish
- Roasted nuts and pumpkin seeds
- A variety of mustards (store in the refrigerator after opening), Tabasco sauce, low-sodium tamari sauce, organic wasabi powder
- Rosewater
- Plum vinegar
- Corn chips
- Homegrown corn for "popcorn"
- Lemongrass, for infusing in tea

How we plan, shop, and eat is part of our healthy-brain lifestyle. Focus on quality and diversity to provide a wide array of essential fats and nutrients to fortify your brain and improve your concentration and mental resilience. What you eat directly affects your daily function, energy, and quality of life at any age. By making sure a whole kaleidoscope of ingredients makes it to your daily food plate, you are off to a great start!

Organic tomato sauce is simple to make and can be frozen so that you always have homemade pasta sauce available in your store cupboards.

Food Preparation

In today's fast-paced world, the acts of preparing food and cooking at home reconnect us with mindfulness, creativity, and patience. By preparing and consuming whole foods from the animal and plant kingdoms, we return to our food cultural roots. It is at this fundamental level that we create healing opportunities by balancing our gut flora, giving us a greater chance to live a happy life filled with vitality. The quality of the food we use, and how we prepare and cook it, is very important, since it has an impact on how available nutrients are to our bodies.

Meat and Fish

Frying, roasting, grilling, and searing protein-rich foods at high temperatures is not recommended, as this destroys nutrients, especially B vitamins. High temperatures produce compounds called advanced glycation end products (AGEs), also called glycotoxins. We absorb these into our bloodstream and they are linked with increased inflammation. This matters when we cook pork, fish, beef, chicken, and eggs, or consume popular steamed drinks with sugary ingredients and artificial flavors. In addition, any browning or blackening of foods, even oozing marshmallows on a stick over a grill or fire, encourages the formation of cancer-causing molecules that can increase inflammation.

All this may sound a bit scary, but there is plenty that you can do to make the most of your food's health benefits. Avoid processed foods with a long expiry date, because they will have been heat-treated to extend their shelf life. Cook meat at a lower temperature for longer: you might steam, sauté, or bake fish or a pork shoulder in a casserole dish, or simmer chicken on the stovetop in a delicious sauce. When using the outdoor grill (barbecue) in the summer, keep the heat medium rather than high, and avoid blackening the meat—your burgers will still be juicy and delicious! Choose heat-stable fats when cooking, such as butter, coconut oil, organic processed olive oil (cold-pressed olive oil is unstable when exposed to heat), avocado oil, ghee, and duck fat. (Oils should not smoke, turn color, or sizzle in the pan.)

Fruit and Vegetables

When consuming organic lemons and oranges (citrus fruits), integrate the peel. It contains limonene, a potent anti-cancer agent. It is limonene that provides a refreshing aroma and taste. Grate the peel over a salad or add it to your shake to awaken the senses. Pesticides and insecticides are stored in the peel of non-organic fruit and vegetables, so do not consume it even if you wash them well. Chop, slice, squeeze, and dice organic vegetables, fruit, and mushrooms to your heart's delight.

Green, yellow, red, white, and orange fruit and vegetables are rich in water-soluble vitamin C and are best blanched or steamed. As soon as they are cooked to your liking, strain them and allow them to cool as desired. The longer green vegetables are left in water, the more they leach out water-soluble vitamins, and the less those vitamins make it into your body.

Top 24 Options for Healthy Food Preparation

Braising	Mincing	Steaming	Pickling
Pan-roasting	Juicing	Simmering	Griddling
Grilling	Blending	Brining	Fermenting
Boiling	Raw foods	Curing	Slow-cooking
Roasting	Blanching	Poaching	Stewing
Pan-frying	Sautéing	Baking	Canning

Grains, Nuts, and Seeds

Phytic acid, an enzyme inhibitor, is in the fiber of grains, legumes, soybeans, nuts, and seeds. It adversely affects the absorption of B12, iron, and zinc from these foods, However, all these nutrients are needed for thyroid, brain, immune and digestive function. The solution is either to reduce your consumption of these foods, or to consider traditional food preparation methods such as fermentation, germination, and soaking to neutralize phytic acid. This unlocks the nutrients that our body can absorb, but it takes time and effort in the kitchen. (Even corn and rice were fermented in traditional cuisines.) Soak nuts, seeds, or grains overnight in a bowl with either sea salt or apple cider vinegar to get rid of the phytic acid. Grains can be cooked in the morning once you have rinsed them well in a strainer (sieve). Rinse nuts, too, in the morning and then lay them out carefully on a dishcloth. Pat them dry as much as you can and put them in the sun to dry for a day (or dry them overnight). You will notice that they are softer, with a more exuberantly nutty flavor. Alternatively, spread out the rinsed nuts or seeds on a baking sheet and put them in the oven at a low temperature until they are fully dried but not roasted. The time they require to dry will depend on their size, so keep an eye on them. It is best to prepare legumes by putting them in a pot filled with water, some sea salt, and a tablespoon of apple cider vinegar. Soak the legumes for 12–24 hours, changing the water three or four times during that period. You will notice that the water is not clear when you rinse the legumes; this shows that the phytic acid is being rinsed off. If you experience gas or bloating after eating beans or lentils, consider increasing the soaking or cooking time, and be sure to rinse them well before cooking.

Fermentation

Fermentation is a traditional method of food preparation that is making a comeback at farmers' markets, restaurants, gourmet stores, and at home. Foods made in this way include the drink known as kombucha, cultured dairy such as kefir, and kimchee. There are various cultured or fermented foods that you can make at home.

Fruit and Vegetables Bite Back!

Raw foods are foods in their purest form. Preparation matters to optimize the bioavailability of nutrients. In addition, plants and fruits have their own defense systems, and some of these can be harmful to humans. Most plant toxins can be neutralized by various cooking methods or fermentation, but with excessive consumption they can still cause trouble for some people, e.g. oxalate crystals associated with gout, or nightshades with osteoarthritis.

Consider the following:

- Goitrogens are found in fruit and vegetables from the cruciferous and brassica families. These plant toxins suppress thyroid function by interfering with the uptake of iodine. Foods that are implicated include broccoli, cauliflower, radishes, horseradish, daikon (mooli), soy, sweet potatoes, turnips, Brussels sprouts, kale, and cabbage. On the flip side, these are nutritious foods, dense in vitamin K, calcium, chlorophyll, vitamin C, fiber, anti-cancer sulforaphane, and many other vital nutrients. It is advisable to neutralize goitrogens by flash-boiling, sautéing, or otherwise cooking these ingredients. With that in mind, do avoid the popular piece of raw cauliflower or broccoli at the next cocktail party and choose raw carrot or celery instead.
- Oxalates (found in spinach, rhubarb, beet greens, chocolate, tea, pecans, coffee, and more) are linked to kidney stones, cataracts, spectrum-related disorders, and headaches. However, if foods high in calcium, such as goat cheese, sardines, bok choy (pak choi), and yogurt, are consumed with high oxalate foods, the calcium and magnesium neutralize oxalates in the intestines, which then are excreted. By incorporating a diverse and nutrient-dense diet, we encourage the body to maintain its unique checks and balances. (It is worth noting that yeast overgowth in the body also encourages oxalate production.)

Choose ripe eggplants (aubergines) when cooking, as they have less solanine, an antifungal chemical, in their skin.

- Plants in the nightshade family, including potatoes, tomatoes, eggplant (aubergine), and peppers of all kinds, contain an antifungal chemical called solanine in their skin to protect against rot. This can create inflammation in sensitive individuals. Solanine levels are highest in unripe fruit and vegetables, so choose ripe and juicy produce for raw salads and cooked meals. This chemical does not degrade with cooking, but some of it is lost in cooking water.
- Certain foods are rich in chemical compounds called salicylates, which are associated with various inflammatory conditions. Salicylates are found in all dried fruit, avocado, oranges, nightshades (see above), strawberries, curry powder, and oregano. Salicylates sensitivity is associated with aspirin intolerance, ADHD, headaches, gastrointestinal disorders, skin problems, asthma, and other respiratory disorders. If you are affected by this, it is best to avoid foods that are high in salicylates, and cook all moderate- to low-salicylate foods thoroughly.

Kitchen equipment

The microwave is best used for disinfecting your kitchen sponge, or drying rain-soaked shoes! Instead of using the microwave, why not consider traditional cooking methods as often as possible? Also avoid Teflon, aluminum, and non-stick pans (even the ceramic non-stick pans that are so popular today), which leach harmful chemicals into foods.

Optimal choices for cooking and baking are:
- Traditional cast-iron cookware, which conducts heat very well, and is durable and good value for money (but avoid acidic foods, including tomatoes, all of which cause the iron to react)
- Copper pots and pans, which also conduct heat very well, but again react with acidic foods
- Ceramic pots for cooking at higher temperatures
- Glass and CorningWare or Pyrex (avoid cheap imitations)
- Stoneware for baking, casseroles, and grilled vegetables
- Stainless steel (although this can leach nickel during cooking)
- A carbon steel wok
- A cooking thermometer

Do invest in sharp knives for meat or poultry, or larger fruit such as melon, Also consider handy 3–4-inch paring knives for vegetables and fruit, and a serrated breadknife that can also be used for slicing tomatoes, peaches, fatty cuts of meat, and sandwiches for the lunchbox. Use knife-friendly wood or bamboo cutting boards for vegetables and fruit, but for cutting or chopping raw meat, poultry, and seafood, use color-coded plastic boards. All boards can harbor harmful bacteria, so make sure to wash them thoroughly; plastic ones can safely go in the dishwasher. For carving cooked meat, invest in an additional board or use the one for vegetables.

Glass cutting boards are attractive and easy to clean but they make your knives dull, so they're not the best choice for the kitchen.

It is best to avoid using aluminum cookware and foil, plastic utensils, or plastic containers for foods that will be exposed to heat. All these things leach chemical hormones called xenoestrogens (which mimic our natural hormones but cause harmful hormone disruption and contribute to problems with estrogen dominance) and other harmful pollutants into warm food and drinks. Toxins accumulate, but even at low levels they can harm our brain. Refrigerate, freeze, or store cooked foods in glass, porcelain, or lead-free ceramic containers, or BPA-free, PVC-free plastic containers.

Final thoughts

Food preparation can take time, but it will serve you well over a lifetime. Making broth (stock) from scratch takes hours, and the scent of a chicken that is roasting in the oven fills the air and makes us hungry way before dinnertime. But it is worth it. We might think our body doesn't care whether we eat home-prepared meals or store-bought foods, but it does know the difference. Our heart and soul are in the meals we prepare in our own kitchen.

On the pages that follow you'll find food preparations that are used in the recipes, but which also are helpful for other things you may be cooking.

Chicken Broth

Broth (stock) is essential in any kitchen.
Whether to heal a leaky gut or to provide
a delicious, warming cup on a cold day,
it is a top brain food for people of all ages.
It is also the base for hearty soups,
whether it is meat- or bone-based.
In a pinch, store-bought broth can be
used, but it is better to make your own.

2 tablespoons butter or olive oil

8¾ lb. (4 kg) chicken wings, or a chicken carcass

2 onions, halved

1 leek, thickly sliced

2 garlic cloves

2 celery sticks, thickly sliced

7 oz. (200 g) button mushrooms, halved

2 carrots, peeled and thickly sliced

a mix of fresh herbs, such as bay leaves, tarragon, parsley,
chervil, and thyme (for a very plain stock, use only parsley)

20 black peppercorns

sea salt

makes about 6 cups (1.5 liters)

Heat the butter or oil in a large pan and add the chicken.
Cook it for a few minutes, without allowing it to color, then
add the onion, leek, and garlic and cook until softened.
Add all the other vegetables to the pan and pour over
3 quarts (liters) of water. Add the fresh herbs and the
peppercorns, cover the pan, and bring to a simmer. Leave
the broth (stock) to simmer for 1½ hours, removing the lid
for the last 30 minutes so that it can reduce a little. Pass
the broth through a fine-mesh strainer (sieve) and/or muslin
(cheesecloth) and discard the solids. Skim the broth if
necessary, adjust the seasoning with salt, and use as per
your recipe.

Dairy-based and Vegan Yogurt

First, try to find a good yogurt starter (live-culture yogurt is readily available from health-food stores or online, or a friend or neighbor might have some to pass on). You can also use store-bought yogurts as starters, but you will need to buy a new one for every third batch or so, because the laboratory-derived cultures are not as strong and stable as traditional cultures. The quality of the milk you use is also important. To make a thick and tasty yogurt, use organic (not ultra-pasteurized) full-cream (whole) milk, and if using coconut milk, use the best-quality organic, unsweetened kind you can find. If you plan to make yogurt in the long term, I suggest finding a supplier (online or locally) of traditional yogurt culture, because it will serve you for many years without losing its effectiveness: simply take a small amount of the yogurt you just made and use it as a starter for the next batch.

4 cups (1 liter) full-cream (whole) milk, preferably sheep or goat, or coconut milk

¼ cup (60 ml) live-culture, plain regular yogurt or coconut yogurt, or 1–2 tablespoons traditional yogurt culture

Makes 4 cups (1 kg)

Make sure the starter is at room temperature. Pour the milk into a heavy pan and heat gently and slowly, whisking frequently, until small bubbles start to form. If you have a cooking thermometer, it should read 175°F (80°C). Allow the milk to cool to 115°F (45°C). If you haven't got a cooking thermometer, dip your finger in the milk after it has been cooling for a few minutes; if it's fairly warm but not hot, it's about right.

Whisk in the starter until fully dissolved. Yogurt cultures need warmth to grow, so keep the mixture warm for 6–12 hours to allow the milk to thicken into a creamy yogurt.

Toward the end of this time, sterilize glass jars by putting them in the oven at 210°F/100°C/Gas ¼ for 10 minutes. Pour the yogurt mixture into the warm jars, seal, and keep in a warm place (ideally at 105–115°F/40–45°C) for 6–12 hours. I place my filled jars in a thermal bag and wrap the bag in a blanket, or heat the oven to 140°F (60°C), put the jars in, switch off the heat (leaving the oven light on), and maintain a constant temperature by checking from time to time and putting the oven on for a couple minutes if necessary. If the temperature is too high, the starter cultures will die, and if it's too low it will take much longer for the yogurt to ferment, making a very runny and mild yogurt drink. All this may seem complicated, but it's just a matter of finding a way to keep the temperature constant and waiting for the starter cultures to do their job. When the time is up, refrigerate and enjoy! Your homemade yogurt will keep for 5 or 6 days.

Water Kefir

Water kefir grains are a symbiotic colony of bacteria and yeast (SCOBY), which feed on sugary water or juice and produce a fizzy liquid that is rich in probiotics. These small translucent granules (sometimes also referred to as tibicos) consist of lactic-acid bacteria and some yeasts, and are actually distinctly different from milk kefir grains, despite the similarity in the names. Like any symbiotic community of bacteria and yeast, water kefir granules need regular feeding if they are to survive. I feed them raw cane sugar, rice syrup, maple syrup, or honey diluted in water, but they will also thrive on agave syrup, any other carbohydrate sweetener, or any sweet liquid (including fruit juice, coconut water, and nut milks). You can also use white sugar, but you'll need to add a pinch of unrefined sea salt to help the water kefir ferment effectively. If you or anyone in your family are a big fan of soda, and want to avoid unhealthy commercially produced drinks, you can make your own fermented probiotic versions with the help of water kefir grains. Depending on the sweetener and fruit you use, you can make many kinds of soda and enjoy the health benefits at the same time.

4 tablespoons water kefir grains

½ cup (100 g) raw cane sugar or other sweetener (see left)

4 cups (1 liter) water, preferably non-chlorinated

2 x 1.5-quart (liter) glass jars with tight-fitting lids

Makes 4 cups (1 liter)

Put the water kefir grains into one of the jars, add the sweetener and water, and stir well. Cover the jar loosely or seal with its lid (I prefer sealing the jar, to get more fizz). Leave the jar to ferment for 48 hours, away from direct sunlight, stirring it on a couple occasions during that time. Taste the liquid: it should be slightly sour. If it's still sweet, leave it to ferment for another 12–24 hours (this might be necessary in winter, or if the temperature in your kitchen is lower than 68°F/20°C). Strain the liquid into a clean jar or bottle, and repeat the feeding process to make another batch.

This fermented drink can be enjoyed immediately or refrigerated for up to a week.

BREAKFAST

Memory-boosting Acai Bowl

Breakfast bowls have become very trendy options for the first meal of the day. Purple, black, and blue fruit improves our cognitive performance and memory. They are full of antioxidants that help to lower inflammation while improving circulation and eyesight. The plant-based sweetener stevia can add a little more sweetness if you choose to forgo the fruit on top.

1 pack frozen acai purée (about ⅓ cup/100 ml)

1 banana, peeled and frozen for about 8 hours

¾ cup (200 ml) almond milk

goji berries and ¼ cup (20 g) unsweetened dried shredded (desiccated) coconut, to serve

strawberries, sliced banana, or sliced kiwi (optional), to serve

Serves 2

Put the acai purée, frozen banana, and almond milk into a food processor and blend until smooth.

Pour the mixture into bowls and sprinkle with goji berries, coconut, and fruit (if using).

VARIATIONS: There are many ways to make this bowlful of goodness. Substitute the acai purée for 5 frozen strawberries and top with extra strawberries and cacao nibs, or use ¼ cup (30 g) frozen blueberries instead of the acai purée and top with sliced kiwi and coconut chips. For an extra-thick fruit base, add an extra frozen banana, or try blending in 2 teaspoons of cacao powder, then top with almond butter and hemp seeds for a chocolate and nut variation. Other fun toppings include a handful of grain-free granola, a dollop of yogurt (such as the Coconut Yogurt on page 52), or crushed seeds and nuts.

Very Berry Brainy Brekkie

I always have some frozen organic berries on hand, but nothing is better than eating freshly picked berries, which help the circulation in our eyes and brain. If you want less sugar, limit the amount of fruit to one portion by using only berries or a banana in your breakfast bowl.

¼ cup (40 g) red and/or yellow raspberries

¼ cup (45 g) blackberries

2 tablespoons red currants

¼ teaspoon umeboshi vinegar

2 cups (500 ml) strained plain (Greek) yogurt (unpasteurized, if available), chilled

1 banana, peeled and cubed

1 tablespoon ground flaxseeds

1 tablespoon pumpkin seeds

1 tablespoon sunflower seeds

Serves 2

Put the raspberries, blackberries, red currants, and umeboshi vinegar in a bowl, crush them lightly with a fork, and leave to stand for 15 minutes. (The vinegar will accentuate the berries' natural sweetness and help them retain their bright colors.)

Divide the fruit mixture and the yogurt between two serving bowls. Add the chopped banana and seeds and serve immediately.

VARIATION: There's a whole world of fruits, seeds, and nuts to choose from. Ring the changes by combining blackberries and apricots with dates and almonds; pears and prunes with sesame seeds; or peaches and grapes with raisins and hazelnuts. I could go on and on ...

Happy Mornin' Warmin' Oatmeal

On a cold winter morning, a bowl of home-cooked oatmeal (porridge) warms the body and heart. I enjoy mine with raw local honey, which boosts the immune system during flu season, and a sprinkling of sea salt on top. Need a dairy-free option? Choose coconut oil, which increases brain energy—it's antiviral, too.

1 cup (130 g) jumbo rolled oats

rice milk (or soy or nut milk)

fresh fruit, such as bananas, berries (fresh or frozen), apples, pears, persimmons, cherries

dried fruit, such as raisins, unsulfured apricots, dates, mango

spices, such as ground ginger, cinnamon, nutmeg

sweeteners, such as agave syrup, pure maple syrup, rice syrup, date syrup, coconut palm sugar (but remember that if you have used a fair amount of fresh and dried fruit, the oatmeal/porridge will be naturally sweet and may not need anything else)

nuts and seeds, such as almonds, cashews, pecans, macadamia nuts, sunflower seeds, hemp seeds, pumpkin seeds, flaxseeds

superfoods, such as goji berries, maca powder, lucuma powder

Serves 2

Put the oats in a pan and cover with half water and half rice milk. Cook gently over a medium-low heat, stirring more and more frequently as it begins to thicken. Oats absorb a huge amount of liquid, so they become thick and gloopy very quickly. Some people love their oatmeal (porridge) at this consistency, but if, like me, you prefer yours a little runnier, just keep adding more rice milk and water until you reach the desired consistency. Only add

---

POWER UP YOUR BRAIN

Goji berries are a tangy red fruit harvested in the Himalayas. They are the only known fruit to contain all eight essential amino acids and provide 15 times more iron than spinach. They contain lutein and zeaxanthin that are known to support eye health, as well as carotenoids that are required for healthy circulation in the brain.

---

a little at a time, though, so you don't overdo it. When it is ready, turn it right down to the lowest heat.

Now add whatever ingredients you like the sound of. My personal favorite combination is banana, raisins, ground cinnamon, pumpkin seeds, goji berries, and the tiniest drop of pure maple syrup. I also love adding frozen blueberries, which defrost in the hot oatmeal, leaving lovely cool pockets of sweetness. The warm oatmeal will have a positive effect on your outlook for the day and your waistline, as well as (ahem) your "regularity" as an added bonus!

Supercharged Sweet Potato, Cavolo Nero, and Plum Tomato Frittata

What a great way to start your day! Free-range egg yolks are power foods filled with vitamin A, vitamin D, B vitamins, and choline, an essential nutrient that helps us to remember, think, and learn. Sulfur-rich onions and garlic detox the brain.

1 sweet potato

extra-virgin olive oil

dried chili flakes

2 red onions, sliced

a handful of ripe baby plum tomatoes

2 tablespoons good balsamic vinegar

a bunch of cavolo nero leaves

10–12 eggs, depending on the size of your pan

a small bunch of fresh basil

1 garlic clove

sea salt and freshly ground black pepper

mixed-leaf salad, to serve

8–10-in. (20–25-cm) ovenproof skillet (frying pan) or quiche dish

Serves 8–10

Preheat the oven to 350°F/180°C/Gas 4.

Cut the potato in half lengthwise and then into thin wedges. Toss in a roasting pan with 2 tablespoons olive oil and a little salt, pepper, and dried chili flakes. Roast in the preheated oven until just browned and starting to blister.

About 15 minutes before the sweet potato is done, toss the red onions and tomatoes on a baking sheet with a few tablespoons of oil, the vinegar, and a sprinkling of salt, and place in the oven. The skins of the tomatoes should be just popping open and the red onions beginning to caramelize when the sweet potato is ready to take out. Leave the oven on.

Strip the cavolo nero leaves from their stalks and blanch the leaves in salted boiling water for about 2 minutes. Drain and refresh in a bowl of cold water.

Crack the eggs into a bowl, season well, and whisk thoroughly.

Place the sweet potato, cavolo nero, tomatoes, and onion (reserving some vegetables for the top) in an ovenproof skillet (frying pan) or quiche dish. Pour the beaten eggs over the top and sprinkle the reserved vegetables on top so that you can see their colors.

Cook in the oven for 25 minutes or until the frittata has puffed up and the top is just firm to the touch.

Meanwhile, finely chop the basil and garlic and mix with 6 tablespoons extra-virgin olive oil to make a loose basil oil.

Allow the frittata to cool a little, then drizzle with the basil oil and serve with a light mixed-leaf salad.

SUPERFOOD: CAVOLO NERO

Cavolo nero, also known as Tuscan kale, is a nutrient powerhouse. It is trendy—there is now a National Kale Day! Various types of kale are filled with brain-protecting phytonutrients including flavonoids, polyphenols, and betacarotene. All improve memory, cognition, and microcirculation. Just 3½ oz. (100 g) provides five times the recommended daily allowance of vitamin A and seven times that of vitamin K, which are needed for healthy skin and bones.

Lovin' My Brain Energizer Muffins

This is a great gluten-free breakfast that packs a protein punch. Cardamom is a staple in East Indian cultures, with its antimicrobial, antidepressant, and aphrodisiac properties. It is also rich in anti-cancer flavonoids, limonene for many digestive disorders, and manganese, which is needed for bone and brain health (but is depleted by glyphosate, the most widely used pesticide in the US and developing countries).

1 cup (125 g) quinoa flour

½ teaspoon baking soda (bicarbonate of soda)

1 teaspoon baking powder

½ teaspoon salt

1 teaspoon ground cardamom

1 teaspoon ground cinnamon

2–3 heaped tablespoons shelled hemp seeds

1–1½ teaspoons orange extract or orange oil

1 tablespoon apple cider vinegar

⅓ cup (85 ml) applesauce (apple purée)

¼ cup (60 ml) rice or almond milk

3 tablespoons pure maple syrup, or more applesauce

2 tablespoons granulated sweetener

24-hole mini-muffin pan or 12-hole regular muffin pan, lined with (eco-friendly) paper cases

Makes 24 mini muffins, or about 9 – 10 regular muffins

Preheat the oven to 350°F/180°C/Gas 4.

In a bowl, combine the quinoa flour, baking (bicarbonate of) soda, baking powder, and salt, then sift in the cardamom and cinnamon. Add the shelled hemp seeds. (There's no need to measure these, really—the more you add, the more protein and healthy fats will be in your muffins.)

In another bowl, mix the orange extract or oil, vinegar, applesauce (apple purée), milk, maple syrup, and sweetener.

Add the wet ingredients to the bowl of dry ingredients and stir together, but be careful not to overmix. Spoon the mixture into the muffin cases, filling them just three-quarters full, and level the tops with your finger or a spoon. Bake in the preheated oven for 8–10 minutes for mini muffins, and 9–12 minutes for regular muffins. It's fine to under-bake these slightly if you want them to be particularly moist on the inside, because none of the ingredients are harmful if consumed raw.

Allow the muffins to cool for 5 minutes before eating. Store in an airtight container for up to 5 days.

Chia Pudding to Keep Attention Humming

This is a fun favorite at any age, be it for breakfast, a mid-afternoon snack, or a dessert. The omega-3 fatty acids and fiber in chia seeds make them a great anti-inflammatory. Three delicious options are given here, but if you use the chia as a base you can play with various milks, fruits, spices, and natural sweeteners, such as raw honey or stevia.

Autumn-spiced Chia Pudding

1 tablespoon chia seeds

6 tablespoons (100 ml) almond milk

freshly squeezed juice of 1 carrot

¼ teaspoon ground ginger

¼ teaspoon ground cloves

¼ teaspoon grated nutmeg

½ teaspoon ground cinnamon

1 tablespoon pure maple syrup, agave syrup, or coconut nectar

Vanilla and Coconut Chia Pudding

1 tablespoon chia seeds

½ cup (125 ml) almond milk

3 tablespoons unsweetened dried shredded (desiccated) coconut

1 teaspoon vanilla extract

Chocolate Chia Pudding

1 tablespoon chia seeds

½ cup (125 ml) almond milk

1½ tablespoons unsweetened cocoa powder

2 tablespoons pure maple syrup

All serve 1

Put the chia seeds and milk into an airtight container and stir well to combine, making sure there are no lumps. Set aside for 10 minutes so that the seeds start to expand.

Add the remaining ingredients, stir again, and refrigerate: for 1 hour if you like it thin, or overnight if you like it thick and comforting, almost like oatmeal (porridge). I put mine in the refrigerator and steal a few spoonfuls when I need a little sweet pick-me-up; it will keep for up to 5 days that way.

POWER UP YOUR BRAIN
Chia means "strength," and this dish provides great brain stamina energy during the day. For the most nutritional benefit, soak them overnight until they become plumpy and soft. Rich in fiber, anti-inflammatory omega-3 oils, protein, and calcium, a delicious bowl of chia pudding prevents spikes and dips in blood sugar and insulin levels. For a low-sugar or low-carb option, choose stevia as a natural sweetener.

2 slices of bread, cut into cubes

6 cooked bacon rashers, broken into pieces (these can be prepared the day before, but make sure they are crispy!)

1 cup (90 g) Cheddar cheese, grated

4 eggs

¼ cup (60 ml) milk or cream

Makes 6

Preheat the oven to 350°F/180°C/Gas 4 and line a 6-hole muffin pan with (eco-friendly) paper cases.

Put the bread cubes in a bowl and add the bacon pieces. Throw in the cheese and give it a good toss so that it's all mixed together. Spoon the mix into the muffin cups, filling each one to the top.

Mix the eggs and milk or cream in a bowl and pour over the bread mixture in each muffin cup, dividing the liquid equally between the cups. You can sprinkle a bit more cheese on the tops if liked.

Bake in the preheated oven for about 15 minutes, until the egg is firmly set. Hit the road.

Ready, Set... Go!

These are great for kids! Life is busy, and sometimes we need a quick breakfast on the go. This power-packed muffin jumpstarts the blood-sugar balance that is needed for learning, focus at work, and stable moods. Low blood sugar is linked to headaches, anxiety, and brain fatigue. (Choose a whole-grain, coconut-flour, or gluten-free bread.)

Calming Low-sugar Cacao Oatmeal

This oatmeal (porridge) is a delight for kids and adults alike. Fermented oats are easy to digest, and cacao is filled with antioxidants, although it can cause headaches for some. Nut butters optimize blood-sugar and insulin response, reducing the risk of type 2 diabetes.

½ cup (50 g) fine rolled oats

2 cups (480 ml) water

pinch of salt

2 tablespoons roasted ground hazelnuts or hazelnut butter

1 tablespoon raw cacao powder

3 tablespoons brown rice syrup or high-quality maple syrup, or to taste

Serves 2

Put the oats in a jar and add the water. Cover loosely with a lid and leave to soak (ferment) for at least 24 hours, or longer.

Pour the soaked oats into a pan, add all the other ingredients except the syrup, and whisk over a medium heat until creamy and bubbly, about 3–5 minutes.

Sweeten to taste with brown rice syrup or maple syrup. I'd advise against making the oatmeal (porridge) too sweet—it's better to save sweets for dessert and serve this oatmeal only mildly sweet with a kick of real cacao taste.

Eggs-cellent Basque Omelet with Peppers and Tomato Sauce

This meal makes a hearty breakfast or lunch. You could add mushrooms to the vegetable medley, or serve free-range bacon on the side. I prefer no sugar in my tomato sauce, but I am generous with garlic, which improves microcirculation in the brain (and lowers blood pressure, too).

For the tomato sauce (makes about 2 cups/500 ml)

2¼ lb. (1 kg) tomatoes

3 tablespoons olive oil

1 large onion

2 garlic cloves, minced

4 tablespoons (60 ml) dry white wine

2 teaspoons herbes de Provence

1 teaspoon fine granulated sugar (optional)

4 tablespoons (60 ml) olive oil

1 medium onion, very thinly sliced

½ medium red bell pepper, deseeded and finely chopped

½ medium green bell pepper, deseeded and finely chopped

6 eggs

salt and freshly ground black pepper

Serves 2

> **POWER UP YOUR BRAIN**
> Egg yolks enhance cognitive function and stable moods, while egg whites provide essential sulfur that is needed in the body to optimize detoxification. And tomato sauce is rich in cancer-protective lycopene that is terrific for heart health.

First make the tomato sauce. Put the tomatoes into boiling water for 30 seconds, drain, and plunge into cold water. The skins will then pull off easily. Keep on one side. (If you can't get fresh tomatoes, good-quality canned tomatoes will do, but drain off the liquid before using.)

Heat the oil in a large skillet (frying pan). Add the onion and garlic, and sauté gently until soft but not brown—about 5 minutes. Add the tomatoes, wine, and herbes de Provence, and simmer gently for 15 minutes, breaking up the tomato flesh. Liquidize with the sugar (if using), return the sauce to the pan, and heat through, turning up the heat and stirring continuously for a few minutes if it isn't thick enough.

For the omelet, heat the olive oil in a large skillet. Add the onion and peppers, cover, and cook gently for 15 minutes, until soft. Using a slotted spoon, take out the vegetables and set aside in a bowl.

Beat the eggs lightly, adding a pinch of salt and freshly ground black pepper. Pour them into the skillet and leave over a low heat until the omelet starts to set and the edges come away from the pan. Add the onion and peppers, then put under the broiler (grill) until the eggs are cooked.

Slide onto a large plate, cut in half, and serve with the tomato sauce.

TIP: You can buy special tomato peelers—like extra-fine vegetable peelers—which will do the job without the need for boiling water.

Quinoa, Fruit, and Cottage Cheese Delight

Ready for a refreshing and filling breakfast bowl or even a light and easy lunch? This bowl of healthy fat, calcium, protein, and fruit is delightful. We know that calcium is needed for bones and teeth, but did you know that it is also needed for electric communication (signaling) in the brain?

½ cup (100 g) cottage cheese

½ cup (175 g) fresh mango, chopped, or ½ cup (60 g) blueberries, strawberries, or raspberries

a sprinkle of hemp heart seeds

⅛ cup (20 g) cooked quinoa

agave nectar, for drizzling

Serves 1

Throw the cottage cheese, fruit, hemp seeds, and quinoa into a bowl and drizzle with a little agave nectar.

Rise and Shine Coconut Yogurt

The brain loves fats, especially the healthy fat found in coconut milk. Chopped nuts add a yummy "crunchy munch" and a hit of fiber, or you could substitute some freshly ground flaxseeds. This delicious yogurt is higher in calories than most, but it will satisfy your appetite and charge your brain while curbing any sugar cravings.

2 x 14-oz. (400-ml) cans full-fat coconut milk

2 probiotic supplement capsules (such as Acidophilus or a broad-spectrum probiotic)

1 heaped teaspoon stevia, to sweeten

1 teaspoon lemon juice

½ cup (60 g) pistachio nuts, roughly chopped

For the Berry Chia Jelly (Jam)

1 cup (140 g) strawberries, chopped

1 cup (120 g) raspberries, chopped

2 teaspoons lemon juice

3 tablespoons ground chia seeds

2 teaspoons stevia

14-oz. (324-ml) sterilized glass jar (see page 9)

Makes 2 cups (16 oz./475 ml) jelly (jam) and serves 2–4

Place the cans of coconut milk in the refrigerator for at least 8 hours, or overnight; this will solidify the healthy coconut fats and separate them from the liquid.

Once chilled, open the cans and carefully scoop off the "cream" that has risen to the top, discarding the liquid at the bottom. Put the coconut cream in a food processor with the contents of the probiotic supplement capsules, the stevia, and the lemon juice. Blend until well combined, then spoon the mixture into the sterilized glass jar. Carefully tap the jar on the counter to get rid of any air pockets, then wipe the jar clean and screw on the lid.

Put the sealed mixture in the oven for 24 hours, with the light on but without actually turning on the heat. This ensures a warm, constant temperature that will encourage fermentation. Next, refrigerate the jar for 3 hours—this is when it will start to thicken.

To make the berry chia jelly (jam), place the strawberries, raspberries, and lemon juice in a pan over a medium heat. Warm through, and when the berries start to soften mash them roughly by hand using a fork or potato masher. Add the ground chia seeds and stir to combine; the mixture will thicken a little. Remove the pan from the heat, add the stevia, and stir until dissolved. Cover and chill in the refrigerator for at least 30 minutes to allow the mixture to set. The jelly can be eaten straight away or stored in a sterilized glass jar or airtight container in the refrigerator for 3–5 days.

Once the yogurt is chilled, serve in small bowls with 2 tablespoons of jelly stirred through and pistachio nuts sprinkled on top. It also goes well with granola or sliced fresh fruit. The yogurt will keep for up to 2 weeks in an airtight container in the refrigerator.

POWER UP YOUR BRAIN

Coconut yogurt is a great source of long-lasting energy, keeping your gut flora diverse and balanced while the brain is humming with steady energy. Lemons are rich in vitamin C that is needed for nerve function and for making brain chemicals including serotonin. Before serving, why not grate a little organic lemon peel over the yogurt for a zingy flair? The peel is rich in limonene, which has anti-cancer properties, reduces high blood pressure, and lessens the risk of stroke. Lemons are a brainfood! Wash the lemon to reduce exposure to pesticides and insecticides— or grow your own, if you can.

POWER UP YOUR BRAIN
Non-starchy eggplant is rich in fiber, copper, vitamin B1, potassium, niacin, folate, vitamin K, and various phytonutrients. These protect our brain cells from harmful molecules associated with oxidation and environmental toxins, while also exhibiting anti-cancer properties.

Psyched-up Eggplant "Bacon" Sandwich

Be it for breakfast or lunch, the creamy avocado is a nutrition-packed addition to any sandwich, smoothie, or salad. Rich in phytonutrients, monounsaturated fat, soluble fiber, and vitamins, it is always welcome on the plate. For a gluten-free sandwich, choose a coconut-flour, sunflower-seed, or pumpkin-seed bread. You will need to make your eggplant "rashers" in advance (see recipe).

For the Eggplant (Aubergine) Bacon

1 large eggplant (aubergine)

1–2 teaspoons sea salt

1 teaspoon liquid smoke (optional)

2 teaspoons smoked paprika

a pinch of chipotle powder

2 tablespoons olive oil

2 tablespoons balsamic vinegar

2 avocados, peeled, pitted (stoned), and roughly chopped

4–8 large slices of raw seed bread (such as Lydia's Organic Sunflower Seed Bread)

2 large tomatoes, sliced

a handful of alfalfa sprouts

dehydrator (optional)

Makes 20–25 "bacon" rashers and serves 4

Begin by preparing the eggplant (aubergine) bacon. If you want the recipe to be raw, you will need a dehydrator for this recipe. If not, an oven is just fine. Preheat the oven or dehydrator to 225°F/110°C/Gas ¼.

Using a mandoline, slice the aubergine (eggplant) into very thin strips and then cut in half lengthwise so that the "rashers" resemble the shape of bacon. If you don't have a mandoline, slice it by hand as thinly as possible, bearing in mind that it needn't be neat. Place the strips in a casserole dish.

Mix the remaining eggplant bacon ingredients together in a small mixing bowl with 6 tablespoons of water. Pour the mixture over the eggplant rashers. Set aside to soften for about 15 minutes.

Remove the eggplant rashers from the dish and place them on a baking sheet or dehydrator sheet, reserving the leftover marinade. Brush lightly with the marinade, then place in the preheated oven or dehydrator. Allow the eggplant bacon to get really crispy—4–6 hours in the oven and 16–20 hours in the dehydrator.

To prepare the ELT sandwiches, lightly mash the avocado onto the seed bread. Top with slices of tomato, the alfalfa sprouts, and 3 or 4 eggplant bacon rashers. You could top with another slice of seed bread or serve as an open sandwich, as shown here. This sandwich is also delicious with a layer of sauerkraut (see page 124). Yum!

LUNCH

Summer Salad with Healthy Fats and Crunchy Seeds

This raw salad is great for vegetarians, or add a sliced grilled chicken breast for the omnivore. It is teeming with linoleic acid, healthy enzymes, vitamins, fiber, and crunchy sprouts.

⅔ cup (100 g) walnuts

⅔ cup (100 g) sunflower seeds

2 celery ribs (stalks), thinly sliced

1 red bell pepper, deseeded and julienned

1 large carrot, julienned

½ cucumber, julienned

a large handful of salad leaves

a handful of alfalfa and sunflower-seed sprouts, or any other variety of sprout

For the mustard dressing
¾ cup (200 ml) safflower oil

¼ cup (60 ml) white wine vinegar

1½ tablespoons Dijon mustard

Himalayan pink salt and freshly ground black pepper

Makes about 1 cup (250 ml) dressing, and serves 4

Soak the walnuts in a bowl of cold water for 2 hours, and the sunflower seeds in a separate bowl of cold water for 30 minutes. Drain thoroughly.

Put the walnuts and sunflower seeds into a food processor and blitz until finely chopped. Transfer to a bowl with the celery, bell pepper, carrot, and cucumber.

For the dressing, put all the ingredients into a screw-top jar and shake well until emulsified. Shake or stir again immediately before serving.

To serve, put the vegetable mixture on a bed of salad leaves, drizzle with the dressing, and sprinkle the sprouts over the top.

4 medium beets (beetroot), cubed

2 cups (500 ml) fresh orange juice

zest of 1 orange, plus orange slices to garnish

5 tablespoons olive oil

¾ cup (75 g) shelled walnuts

10 radishes, washed and thinly sliced

sea salt

Serves 4

Wash the beets (beetroot) and cut off the tops, leaving about an inch of stem. Place them, unpeeled, in a pan and pour in enough boiling water to half-cover them. Simmer, covered, until tender—about an hour. Allow to cool, then rub off the skins.

Season the beets with a little salt, dice them, and put them into another pan. Add the orange juice, zest, and olive oil and simmer gently for 10 minutes. Increase the heat and boil until most of the liquid has evaporated. Meanwhile, dry-fry the walnuts in a skillet (frying pan) until they are just turning brown, about 2 minutes. Serve the beets in their juice, sprinkled with the walnuts and radishes.

TIP: Beets can stain hands and plastic boards and utensils, so wear gloves and use glass or stainless-steel bowls and pans.

Vitamin-rich Beet, Orange, Radish, and Walnut Salad

A tantalizing salad rich in gallbladder- and liver-friendly ingredients. Radishes of all colors stimulate the flow of bile, which detoxifies the brain and contributes to weight loss. Beets (beetroot) cleanse the blood while providing sweetness. Do save the beet tops and use them in a smoothie, or add to another meal by sautéing them in olive or coconut oil.

Omega-3 Filled Smoked Salmon with Lentils, Onions, and Carrots

Wild salmon is rich in astaxanthin, which gives salmon its color and encourages good circulation in the eye and brain. Do avoid commercially farmed salmon. The fish are raised in enclosed ocean pens and fed GMO food pellets, colorants, dyes from petrochemicals, growth hormones, and antibiotics. It is best to buy wild salmon of Alaskan origin.

2 tablespoons (¾ oz./25 g) unsalted butter

2 tablespoons canola (rapeseed) oil

1 large red onion, chopped

1 large carrot, peeled and diced

1¼ cups (250 g) green Puy lentils, washed thoroughly and drained

1¾ cups (400 ml) vegetable broth (stock)

1 bouquet garni

1 tablespoon balsamic vinegar

4 fl. oz. (125 ml) low-fat plain yogurt

4 slices of organic smoked salmon

a small bunch of chives

sea salt and freshly ground black pepper

Serves 4

Melt the butter and oil in a heavy pan over a low heat. Sweat the onion and carrot in the pan until soft but not brown—about 10 minutes. Add the lentils, stir well to coat, and cook for another 10 minutes. Pour in just enough broth (stock) to cover them, and simmer for 20 minutes. Add the bouquet garni, a pinch of salt, and plenty of pepper, and simmer for another 15 minutes, or until the lentils are just cooked. Strain and leave to cool, covered.

Whisk the vinegar and yogurt together in a bowl and season lightly. To serve, arrange the lentils on an oval platter, pour on the yogurt dressing, place rolled slices of salmon on top, and decorate with the chives.

POWER UP YOUR BRAIN
Wild salmon is also rich in vitamin D, omega-3 fatty acids, selenium, vitamin B12, iodine, and other nutrients, all of which feed the brain and decrease the risk of ADHD, dementia, Alzheimer's, and Parkinson's disease.

Anti-aging Silky Asparagus Soup with Sour Cream and Chives

This fresh-tasting asparagus soup is a great source of vitamins A, C, K, and B6. With its powerful diuretic properties, asparagus also calms symptoms that affect the urinary tract, while easing the fluid retention associated with hormonal fluctuations. (Do avoid asparagus if you have gout, though.)

3½ tablespoons (50 g) butter

6 banana (or other sweet) shallots, diced

8 new potatoes, peeled and diced

3⅓ cups (800 ml) vegetable or chicken broth (stock)

1½ bunches of asparagus spears

7 tablespoons (100 ml) heavy (double) cream and sour cream combined (for a little more "edge," use all sour cream, or for a richer soup use all heavy/double cream)

sea salt and freshly ground black pepper

freshly snipped chives, to serve

Serves 4–6

Melt the butter in a large pan and add the shallots and potatoes. Toss them in the butter and cook very gently so that they take in some of the butter, but do not allow them to color. Pour over the broth (stock), cover, and simmer for about 15 minutes, until the potatoes are tender.

Snap the woody ends off the asparagus spears. (Breaking them at the point at which they are naturally inclined to snap means you remove any woody, fibrous stalk, which isn't good for the soup.) Roughly chop the spears and add them to the pan. Cook for a few more minutes only, so that they retain their vibrant green color. When the asparagus is almost tender, remove the pan from the heat and blend the soup with a stick blender, adding the cream a little at a time as you blend, to give the soup a silky finish. Season to taste with salt and freshly ground black pepper.

Ladle the soup into bowls, garnish with freshly snipped chives, and serve immediately.

Nourish with Quinoa, New-season Beans, Peas, and Asparagus

This is a light and family-friendly summer lunch or picnic food—and the protein-rich leftovers are delicious, too! Switch it up with homemade broth (stock), or just use sea salt and water for a vegetarian option. For less sugar, skip the agave, and allow the flavour of the fresh herbs and green veggies to blossom.

1½ cups (300 g) quinoa

2 teaspoons bouillon (stock) powder

12 asparagus spears, cut in half

2 cups (200 g) shelled fava (broad) beans

2 cups (200 g) peas

a large handful of fresh mint

a handful of fresh parsley

a handful of cherry tomatoes, halved

grated zest and juice of 1 lemon

¾ cup (200 ml) extra-virgin olive oil, plus extra for drizzling

2 tablespoons agave syrup

1 tablespoon pomegranate molasses or balsamic vinegar

sea salt and freshly ground black pepper

Serves 6

Put the quinoa and bouillon (stock) powder in a pan and cover with just under double its volume of water. Bring to the boil, then reduce the heat to low and cover with a lid. Cook for about 12 minutes, or until all the water has been absorbed. Turn off the heat, remove the lid, and let any remaining water evaporate. Remove the quinoa to a wide plate or tray and leave to cool.

Meanwhile, bring a pan of water to the boil (just enough to cover each set of vegetables you are cooking) and add 2 teaspoons salt. Cook the asparagus, beans, and peas separately until just tender—about 3–4 minutes for each. You still want them to have some bite.

Once the beans are cooked, you will need to remove their outer cases. This is a bit time-consuming, but the result is truly worth it, for the color if for nothing else. I like to delegate to family or friends who might be joining me for dinner, and this is the perfect job for them! Simply slide the pale case off each bean and discard.

Roughly chop the herbs and reserve some for serving. In a large bowl, mix the quinoa, asparagus, beans, peas, tomatoes, and remaining herbs gently but thoroughly. Add the lemon zest and juice, oil, agave syrup, molasses, salt, and pepper. Mix again, taste, and adjust the seasoning if necessary.

Serve in a large dish with the reserved herbs sprinkled on top. Finish off with a drizzle of olive oil.

SUPERFOOD: QUINOA

1 cup (200 g) of quinoa provides 3 g more protein than the average egg. It also supplies all eight of the essential amino acids, so it is a complete protein for vegetarians and meat-eaters alike. This nutritious and fiber-rich meal is terrific for blood-sugar balance, which enhances great focus and happy moods during a busy day.

Healthy and Hearty Soup to Warm the Soul, Heart, and Brain

This homemade soup can be your go-to during colder months—you can freeze it to enjoy whenever the family needs a warming, hearty meal. The options are endless. Substitute veggies for whatever lingers in your refrigerator, and, instead of ground (minced) beef, consider ground lamb.

2–3 tablespoons vegetable oil

9 oz. (250 g) ground (minced) beef

1 small onion, diced

2 large garlic cloves, crushed

½ rutabaga (swede), peeled and diced

1 small carrot, peeled and diced

½ celery root (celeriac), peeled and diced

2 celery ribs (stalks), sliced

1 small leek, white only, sliced

1 small potato, peeled and diced

14-oz. (400-g) can chopped tomatoes

3½ cups (800 ml) beef broth (stock)

4 generous tablespoons (60 g) tomato paste (purée)

1¾ cups (250 g) peas, fresh or frozen

a small bunch of fresh parsley, chopped, plus extra to garnish

a few sprigs of fresh thyme

a splash of Worcestershire sauce (optional)

sea salt and freshly ground black pepper

Serves 6

Melt the oil in a large, heavy pan. Add the beef and fry until browned, stirring all the time to brown the meat evenly. Add the onion and garlic and continue to cook until the onion is translucent and softened.

Add all the vegetables and stir them into the meat and onions, making sure there is no clumping of any one ingredient—you want them all evenly dispersed. Add the chopped tomatoes, beef broth (stock), and tomato paste (purée), and cover with a lid. Simmer gently for about 12 minutes, or until the vegetables are almost soft but still a little al dente. Now add the peas and herbs and season with salt and black pepper. If you want a little extra flavor, add a splash of Worcestershire sauce and simmer for a few more minutes to let all the flavors marry, before spooning into warmed bowls, to serve.

TIP: If you are not eating the soup immediately, the peas are better added just before the soup is required, so that they retain their lovely green color. This soup is perfect served with delicious multigrain bread and unsalted butter.

Up Your Focus with Beets, Cherry Tomatoes, and Soft-boiled Eggs on Rye Bread

Beets (beetroot) nourish our blood and our liver. With their blood-cleansing and energy-boosting properties, beets and their nutrient-rich green tops are a versatile salad ingredient. Although high in sugar, they are also abundant in fiber, vitamin C, betaine, folate, and naturally occurring nitrites that have anti-inflammatory properties.

10 oz. (300 g) large beets (beetroot), topped, tailed, and cut into ¾-in. (2-cm) wedges (leave the skin on)

2 teaspoons olive oil

10 oz. (300 g) new potatoes

3 eggs

½ small red onion, thinly sliced

2 tablespoons extra-virgin olive oil, plus extra to serve

1 teaspoon wholegrain mustard

4 slices of rye bread, cut lengthways

1 garlic clove, peeled and halved

a handful of arugula (rocket)

12 cherry tomatoes, halved

1 scallion (spring onion), thinly sliced

sea salt and freshly ground black pepper

Serves 4

Preheat the oven to 350°F/180°C/Gas 4. In a roasting pan, toss the beet (beetroot) wedges with the olive oil, and season. Roast for 30–35 minutes, or until tender and the skins are beginning to blister. Turn the oven off, but leave the beets in to keep warm.

In a pan, cover the potatoes generously with cold, salted water. Bring to the boil and simmer briskly for 10 minutes. Add the eggs to the pan and simmer for another 6–7 minutes. Remove the eggs with a slotted spoon and plunge into ice-cold water. Cook the potatoes for a further few minutes until tender. Drain, then cut them in half roughly while still warm. Combine the potatoes with the red onion, 1 tablespoon of extra-virgin olive oil, and the wholegrain mustard; season and set aside.

Toast the bread and while still hot rub generously with the cut side of the garlic, almost grating it against the rough surface of the toasted bread. Divide the bread between four plates, drizzle over another tablespoon of olive oil, and sprinkle with sea salt.

Place a few leaves of arugula (rocket) on top of the toast, then tumble over some potatoes, beets, and tomatoes. Finish with the soft-boiled eggs, peeled and cut into wedges, and sprinkle over the scallions (spring onions). Season again, if needed, and drizzle over a little more oil. Serve immediately.

Fortify: Chicken Liver Pâté

Liver from grass-fed animals and chickens is the most nutrient-dense food for our body. It provides excellent and bioavailable sources of vitamins A, D, B12, folate, iron, trace minerals, and Co10 that we need for energy production. Liver gives us energy and fortifies us at any age, especially after illness.

3 tablespoons (45 g) butter

2 shallots, finely chopped

1 garlic clove, chopped

3 oz. (75 g) rindless pork belly, diced

7 oz. (200 g) chicken livers, chopped

1 teaspoon freshly chopped thyme, plus a few leaves to garnish

1 tablespoon brandy

1 bay leaf

freshly squeezed lemon juice, to taste

salt and freshly ground black pepper

black and pink peppercorns, to garnish (optional)

whole-wheat (wholemeal) toast, to serve

4 x 5-oz. (150-ml) ramekins or similar small ovenproof dishes

Serves 4

Melt half the butter in a skillet (frying pan) over a medium heat. Add the shallots and garlic and fry for 1 minute.

Add the pork belly, chicken livers, chopped thyme, brandy, and a pinch each of salt and pepper, and stir well.

Add the bay leaf to the mixture. Cook for 10 minutes, stirring, until everything is browned and the chicken livers and pork are cooked through.

Remove the pan from the heat and leave to cool until the mixture is warm but not hot.

Remove and discard the bay leaf. Transfer the mixture to a food processor (don't wash the skillet just yet, you'll use it again). Add a squeeze of lemon juice to the mixture and whizz until blended. It's up to you how smooth you want it. I like it quite smooth, but you can keep it coarse by stopping just as the mixture starts to stick to the sides of the processor.

Spoon the mixture into the ramekins, leaving about ¼ in. (5 mm) at the top. Melt the rest of the butter in the original skillet over a medium heat, until it starts to bubble. Take the pan off the heat and carefully pour the butter over the top of each ramekin of pâté. Decorate with a sprinkling of thyme leaves and some black and pink peppercorns, if using.

Transfer the ramekins to the refrigerator and allow at least an hour for the butter to set before serving with whole-wheat (wholemeal) toast. The pâté will keep for up to 9 days in the refrigerator if the seal is unbroken. Eat within 3 days if you break the butter. You can also freeze the pâté in the ramekins for up to 3 months (before sealing with butter) by wrapping each one in plastic wrap (cling film). If you do this, it's best to defrost them in the refrigerator slowly overnight, rather than with any heat or microwaving. You can still pour melted butter on top after defrosting, or just enjoy them without it.

Sesame Chicken Wraps with Brain-healthy Fats

This great gluten-free option is light, easy to prepare, and delicious. A variety of colored vegetables, chicken or turkey (or you could use grilled fish), and a variety of herbs are brought together with an avocado and tahini dressing for a delicious summer lunch.

Put all the dressing ingredients into a food processor or blender and blitz until smooth. If it seems too thick, add a little more water, but you don't want it to run out of your wrap. Set aside.

Cut the chicken or turkey into strips so that it will cook quickly and thoroughly. Put the sesame seeds in a small, shallow bowl and mix in the yeast or hemp seeds, if using. Dip the meat in the seeds so that it is coated all over.

Heat a skillet (frying pan) with the olive oil and add the meat. Fry on each side until lightly browned and cooked through.

To assemble the wraps, lay the chicken on the lettuce leaves, add the vegetables, and pour the dressing over the top. Roll up and enjoy!

For the dressing

¼ cup (50 g) light or dark tahini

a handful of fresh cilantro (coriander)

½ avocado, chopped

juice of 1 lime

1 teaspoon freshly grated root ginger

⅛ cup (35 g) runny honey

½ cup (120 ml) water

For the wraps

2 boneless turkey or chicken breasts

½ cup (70 g) sesame seeds

2 tablespoons nutritional yeast or 2 tablespoons hemp seeds (optional)

olive oil

large lettuce leaves, washed, for wrapping

2 carrots, cut into thin sticks

1 small to medium cucumber, cut into thin sticks

½ cup (70 g) snow peas (mangetout), cut into thin sticks

Serves 3 or 4 as a light meal

Satisfying Veggie Spaghetti with Tapenade

Who doesn't like spaghetti? This is a delicious summer dish, and the anchovies give it an extra tang. They may be an acquired taste, but they are a source of niacin, which wards off cognitive decline. Zippy zucchini (courgette) is rich in potassium, which can prevent muscle cramping. In addition, zucchini is rich in vitamin C, and in vitamin A, which boosts the heart, brain, and eyes. Any extra tapenade can be refrigerated for up to a week and used in other dishes.

For the spaghetti

4 medium yellow or green zucchini (courgettes)

4–6 tablespoons olive oil

2 tablespoons finely ground almonds

½ cup (60 g) pine nuts (optional)

sea salt

For the tapenade

8 salt-packed anchovies, soaked in cold water for about 20 minutes

½ cup (80 g) cured green olives, pitted (stoned) and chopped

1 tablespoon capers, rinsed and chopped

2 small onions, finely diced

2 garlic cloves, crushed

¼ cup (60 ml) olive oil

½ cup (50 g) chopped fresh parsley

1–2 tablespoons freshly squeezed lemon juice

spiralizer (optional)

Serves 4

Peel the zucchini (courgettes) and use the spiralizer to make "spaghetti." If you don't have a spiralizer, cut the zucchini lengthways into very thin slices, then cut those into very narrow strips.

Sprinkle a little salt over the "spaghetti," then leave to stand for 5 minutes. Dry it well with paper towels (kitchen paper). Toss with the olive oil and ground almonds, to prevent the spaghetti from being too slippery and to help it hold the sauce better.

For the tapenade, drain the anchovies, then bone and chop them. Mix together all the ingredients and leave to stand for at least 15 minutes.

Divide the "spaghetti" among four bowls and top each helping with tapenade just before serving. Drizzle a little more olive oil over the top if you like, and garnish with pine nuts, if using. Enjoy your healthy spaghetti!

3 kale leaves, stripped from the stalks

6-in. (15-cm) piece of cucumber

½ red bell pepper

1 teaspoon freshly grated root ginger

freshly squeezed juice of 1 lemon

1 avocado, peeled and pitted (stoned)

1 cup (250 ml) coconut water

1 medium tomato, halved

4 tablespoons chopped fresh dill, plus extra to serve

1 garlic clove

¼ onion

½ teaspoon salt

olive oil and freshly ground black pepper, to serve

Serves 2

Green Energy Soup

This homemade soup is overflowing with phytonutrients—and has none of the processed salt, preservatives, and additives of store-bought soups. Phytonutrients in plants and fruit are involved in many biochemical processes in the body. They assist in our daily detox, protecting us from inflammation associated with heavy metal accumulation, pesticides, and excessive environmental pollutants.

Put all the ingredients except the olive oil and black pepper into a blender and blitz at low speed until completely smooth. Transfer the mixture to a small pan set over a medium heat and warm through.

Pour into serving bowls, drizzle with olive oil, sprinkle with black pepper and a few extra sprigs of dill, and serve immediately.

DINNER

Immune-boosting Chicken Tikka Masala

I grew up in South Africa, so I love eating a good curry with lots of spices, and sliced banana on the side. Spices, chile peppers, garlic, and onion create a healing medley with their individual medicinal properties. Improve circulation and digestion, lower inflammation, and awaken your taste buds with this simply delicious dish!

4 teaspoons olive oil

1 red onion, diced

1 garlic clove, finely chopped

4 chicken breasts (or 2 breasts and 2 boneless thighs), diced

1 red chile, deseeded and finely chopped

a pinch each of ground ginger, ground turmeric, ground cumin, and paprika

freshly squeezed juice of ½ lime (the rest can be cut into wedges, to serve)

3 tablespoons tomato paste (purée)

a large pinch of chopped cilantro (coriander), plus extra whole leaves to garnish

1 teaspoon soft dark brown sugar

7 oz. (200 g) can chopped tomatoes

5 tablespoons heavy (double) cream

sea salt and freshly ground black pepper

cooked basmati rice and naan bread, to serve

Serves 4

Heat the oil in a pan over a high heat and fry the onion and garlic for about 5 minutes, until they start to brown.

Add the diced chicken, the chile, all the pinches of scrummy seasoning, a pinch of salt and pepper, and the lime juice (if you cut the lime lengthways, you can make longer wedges and leave the other half to serve—it's easier to squeeze).

Stir in the tomato paste (purée), cilantro (coriander), and sugar. Lastly, add the chopped tomatoes and cream.

Bring to the boil, then reduce the heat to low and simmer for 15–20 minutes, until the chicken is cooked through.

Taste and check the seasoning. A good trick is to taste the sauce and then smell each of the seasonings—your nose will tell you whether you want to add a pinch more of anything, or just a little salt and pepper.

Serve with rice and naan bread, and a sprinkling of extra cilantro leaves.

Chicken Tagine with Superfood Ginger, Green Olives, and Preserved Lemon

When I was a child, my family fought over the chicken legs! This Moroccan-inspired roast chicken adds an extra dimension with its pungent flavors of saffron, ginger, cinnamon, and lemon. In ancient times, valuable saffron was used to treat coughs, colds, heart trouble, and stomach ailments.

3 garlic cloves, crushed

a bunch of fresh cilantro (coriander), finely chopped, plus extra to garnish

freshly squeezed juice of 1 lemon

1 teaspoon sea salt

1 whole organic chicken, roughly 2¾ lb. (1.3 kg)

3–4 tablespoons olive oil

1 large onion, grated

a generous pinch of saffron threads

1½ oz. (40 g) fresh root ginger, peeled and grated

1 teaspoon freshly ground black pepper

2 cinnamon sticks

2 teaspoons coriander seeds

1 generous cup (175 g) cracked green olives

rind of 1 preserved lemon, cut into thin strips

2 tablespoons (25 g) butter

1–2 tablespoons runny honey

crusty bread or couscous, to serve

Serves 4–6

Mix together the garlic, cilantro (coriander), lemon juice, and salt, then rub into the cavity of the chicken. Mix the olive oil with the grated onion, saffron, ginger, and black pepper and rub the mixture over the outside of the chicken. Cover and leave to stand for about 30 minutes.

Place the chicken in a large tagine or a heavy casserole pot. Pour any leftover marinade juices over it and add enough water to come almost halfway up the chicken. Add the cinnamon sticks and coriander seeds, place over a high heat, and bring the water to the boil. Reduce the heat, cover with the lid, and simmer for about an hour, turning the chicken over from time to time.

Meanwhile, preheat the oven to 350°F/180°C/Gas 4.

Lift the chicken out of the tagine or casserole pot and place it on a board. Quickly, turn up the heat under the tagine and boil the cooking liquid to reduce it. Stir in the olives and preserved lemon and keep reducing the liquid until it just covers the base of the tagine. Season to taste.

Put the chicken back in the tagine, baste it thoroughly with the cooking juices, dot the top of the chicken with small pieces of butter, and drizzle with the honey. Roast the chicken for 15–20 minutes in the preheated oven until it is golden brown. Garnish with cilantro and serve immediately, with crusty bread or couscous to mop up the tangy, buttery juices.

POWER UP YOUR BRAIN
Rosemary is an evergreen plant in the mint family and is used for both culinary and medicinal purposes. It contains substances that are useful for stimulating circulation in the brain, antimicrobial activities in the gut, lowering allergic responses to foods, improving digestion, and lowering inflammation in the brain. Besides its flavorful aroma in foods, it awakens the senses and induces a sense of calm and wellbeing.

Awaken the Senses: Rosemary Shish Kebabs

This colorful plant-based medley "on a stick" is a delightful summer meal, not to mention a great party option. Make sure you plan ahead to allow the flavorful, immune-boosting rosemary and garlic marinade to fully enhance this dish. Tempeh, a fermented food, is a satisfying protein choice.

1 red and 1 yellow bell pepper

14 oz. (400 g) tempeh

1 large zucchini (courgette)

10 oz. (300 g) small button mushrooms

2 onions, peeled and cut into wedges

10 medium cauliflower florets

10 medium broccoli florets

at least 16 long, thick rosemary stems

freshly ground black pepper

halved cherry tomatoes and salad leaves, such as arugula (rocket), watercress, mustard leaves, and cress, to serve

For the marinade

6 sun-dried tomatoes, soaked in warm water for about an hour

4 garlic cloves, peeled

½ tablespoon fresh rosemary needles

2 teaspoons dried oregano

2 teaspoons dried basil

¼ cup (60 ml) olive oil, plus extra for oiling

¼ cup (60 ml) tamari soy sauce

3 tablespoons freshly squeezed lemon juice

1 teaspoon ginger juice

Serves 4

Remove the seeds from the bell peppers. Chop the peppers, tempeh, and zucchini (courgette) into ¾-in. (2-cm) cubes. Discard the stems of the mushrooms and wipe the caps with a piece of paper towel (kitchen paper).

To make the marinade, put all the ingredients into a food processor and blitz to a thin sauce, adding a little water. Season to taste with black pepper.

Place all the vegetables and the tempeh in a shallow bowl and pour the marinade over them. Mix well and allow to marinate for a couple of hours or overnight, stirring occasionally during that time, if possible.

Wash the rosemary sprigs well and strip off the needles, leaving a ¾-in. (2-cm) tuft at the bottom of each stem. These will be the skewers.

Oil the skewers lightly with olive oil. Skewer the marinated ingredients alternately along the rosemary stems. You should have about 16 fully loaded kebabs.

Put the kebabs on a bed of spicy young leaves, such as arugula (rocket), watercress, mustard leaves, and cress, and add some halved cherry tomatoes. If there's any marinade left, drizzle it over the skewers. Serve immediately.

Sustenance with Smoked Mackerel Sushi Rolls

What a nutrient-dense meal for any dinner plate! Seaweed contains iodine, which is essential for the thyroid, liver, skin, and reproductive organs. (Iodine deficiency is associated with mental retardation in children.) Mackerel is jam-packed with omega-3 oils, which are known for their inflammation-busting properties.

1¼ cups (255 g) brown or white sushi rice

3 tablespoons (50 ml) mirin (sweetened rice wine)

5 nori seaweed sheets

black sesame seeds

12 oz. (350 g) smoked mackerel, cut into thin strips

2 scallions (spring onions), cut into thin strips

½ red bell pepper, cut into thick strips

wasabi, pickled ginger, and light soy sauce, to serve

bamboo sushi mat

Serves 4

Wash the sushi rice thoroughly under cold running water and drain well. Place in a pan and add 2⅓ cups (550 ml) water. Bring to the boil, uncovered, then turn the heat right down and simmer gently until nearly all the water has been absorbed (20–25 minutes). Remove the pan from the heat, place the lid on top, and leave it to stand for 15 minutes to absorb the last of the water.

Spread the rice out on a clean baking sheet and drizzle with the mirin, turning it with a spatula to help it cool down.

While it is cooling, wrap the bamboo sushi mat in plastic wrap (cling film), squeezing out any trapped air. This helps to prevent the rice from sticking. Lay the mat lengthwise in front of you. Take one nori sheet and lay it, shiny side down, on the bamboo mat. Wet your hands and take a small handful of rice. Starting at the far end, spread and pat the rice across the nori sheet, leaving a ½-in. (¼-cm) gap along the edge of the sheet closest to you. You can add more rice if needed, but keep it even and no more than ½ in. (1 cm) thick. If it starts sticking to your hands, simply wet them again. You can also use the back of a spoon dipped in water.

Sprinkle black sesame seeds over the rice, then flip the nori sheet over so that the rice is facing downward, with the edge free of rice still closest to you and in line with the edge of the bamboo mat. Lay three lines of mackerel, scallion (spring onion), and red bell pepper across the middle of the nori.

Then, using the bamboo mat, roll the edge of the nori sheet closest to you over the filling in the middle, tucking it over firmly so the filling is enclosed. When it looks as though you are about to roll the mat into the sushi roll, pull the mat back and continue to roll, applying even pressure and tightening as you go, using the mat to shape the roll. Once the roll has come together, take it carefully off the mat, lay the mat over it, and press and smooth the roll, compressing it tightly and evening out the ends. The roll will actually be more of a rectangular shape when you have finished. With a sharp, wet knife, cut the roll in half and then cut each half into three or four even pieces.

Repeat with the remaining ingredients.

Arrange the rolls on a plate with a mound of wasabi and pickled ginger, and serve the soy sauce in a small dish on the side.

Cognition-boosting Coconut and Lamb Soup

If there ever was an anti-inflammatory "home run," this is it! Coconut is an energy-booster for the brain, cumin is an anti-inflammatory spice that packs a tasty punch, and lamb chunks are an excellent source of protein and B vitamins, including niacin, riboflavin, and B12, which are needed for the production of red blood cells.

Heat the oil in a large, heavy pan and add the onions and lamb. Cook over a medium-high heat until the lamb is sealed and turning an even brown. Add the garlic, chile, ginger, and all the dried spices, and cook over a medium heat for a few more minutes, until the lamb has absorbed all the spices.

Add the broth (stock), coconut milk, and passata, cover the pan, and cook very gently for 40–50 minutes, until the lamb is almost tender. Stir in the lentils and continue cooking over a low heat for a further 15 minutes, until the soup is thickened and the lentils are cooked. Season with salt and pepper, and add a little more chili powder if you would like more heat. Finally, lift the flavor with a little lemon juice.

To make the raita, stir together the mint, yogurt, and cucumber.

Just before serving, gently stir the baby spinach leaves into the soup, to wilt them, then ladle the piping hot soup into large bowls. Sprinkle with the cilantro (coriander) leaves and almonds and serve with the raita on the side (or swirl a little into the soup, if you prefer).

4 tablespoons vegetable oil or ghee

2 onions, thinly sliced

1¾–2¼ lb. (750 g–1 kg) lamb (leg, rump, or shoulder), cut into bite-sized pieces

2 garlic cloves, crushed

2 red chiles, deseeded and sliced

1-in. (2.5-cm) piece of fresh root ginger, peeled and grated

½ tablespoon ground cumin

1½ tablespoons garam masala

½ tablespoon ground coriander

about 1 teaspoon chili powder

2 teaspoons ground turmeric

8 green cardamom pods

1 teaspoon ground cloves

4 cups (1 liter) chicken or vegetable broth (stock)

14-oz. (400-ml) can coconut milk

1 cup (250 ml) passata

1 cup (200 g) red or green lentils

a squeeze of lemon juice

1 lb. (500 g) baby spinach leaves

a handful of fresh cilantro (coriander), roughly chopped

1 cup (100 g) slivered (flaked) almonds, toasted

sea salt and freshly ground black pepper

For the raita
a bunch of fresh mint leaves, finely chopped

¾ cup (200 g) plain yogurt (sheep is best)

½ cucumber, grated

Serves 6–8

Quinoa with Aromatic Mint, Orange, and Beet

This delicious salad is full of refreshing flavors to satisfy the palate. Quinoa, a sacred food from South America, is rich in protein and carbohydrates and has an earthy, nutty flavor. After cooking, rinse it well to wash away any phytic acid residue, which inhibits thyroid function.

4 beets (beetroot) (about 14 oz./400 g total weight), scrubbed clean

extra-virgin olive oil

1 tablespoon balsamic vinegar

1½ cups (300 g) quinoa

1 teaspoon fennel seeds

1 teaspoon cumin seeds

2 oranges

zest of 1 lemon

a large handful of fresh mint leaves, chopped, plus extra for serving

a small handful of fresh flat-leaf parsley leaves, chopped

sea salt and freshly ground black pepper

Serves 4–6

Preheat the oven to 400°F/200°C/Gas 6.

Trim the beet (beetroot) stalks, leaving about 1 in. (2.5 cm) on the top. Cut the beets into wedges about ¾ in. (2 cm) thick, toss in 2 teaspoons of olive oil, and season with salt and pepper. Place in a roasting pan and roast for 30–40 minutes, until blistered and a sharp knife slides into the flesh easily. Remove from the oven and toss with the balsamic vinegar while still hot.

Put the quinoa into a pan over a medium heat with just under double its volume of salted water. The moment it comes to the boil, reduce the heat to low and cover with a lid. Cook for about 12 minutes, or until all the water has been absorbed. Turn off the heat, remove the lid, and let any remaining water evaporate. Remove to a wide plate or tray and leave to cool.

Place the fennel and cumin seeds in a dry skillet (frying pan) over a medium heat for a few minutes, until aromatic. Turn off the heat.

Grate the zest of one orange and set aside. Cut the top and bottom off both oranges, just down to the flesh, then place the oranges on their ends, cut side down. Carefully, following the shape of the orange, cut the skin off in strips from top to bottom, removing all the pith as well. Then segment the oranges by cutting the flesh away from the membrane. Reserve the juice that has come out during preparation.

In a large bowl, combine the quinoa with the orange zest, lemon zest, spices, and chopped herbs, and season to taste with salt and pepper. Add most of the beet and orange segments (and reserved juice), and a little extra-virgin olive oil. Combine and serve at room temperature with the remaining beet and orange segments on top and a few fresh mint leaves sprinkled over.

Keep the Brain On Guard with Sea Bass, Cauliflower Purée, and Swiss Chard

Wild fish packs a lot of power as a great source of protein, abundant iodine for the thyroid, and omega-3 oils, which are anti-inflammatory for the brain. Add cauliflower with its anti-cancer properties, garlic to improve microcirculation, and Swiss chard with vitamins A and K for a nutrient-packed meal.

extra-virgin olive oil, for frying

1 onion, diced

4 garlic cloves, crushed

1 head of cauliflower, cut into florets (about 1 lb./450 g)

scant 4 cups (800 ml) vegetable broth (stock), or enough to cover

a bunch of Swiss chard, about 14 oz. (400 g), leaves separated from the thick stalks

4 sea bass fillets

a small bunch of fresh flat-leaf parsley, finely chopped

sea salt and freshly ground black pepper

Serves 4

Pour 2 tablespoons of olive oil into a large skillet (frying pan) over a medium heat. Add the onion and sweat for 10 minutes until soft. Add almost all of the garlic and cook for a minute, then add the cauliflower, stir everything together, and cook for 2 minutes more.

Pour in enough vegetable broth (stock) just to cover the cauliflower. Bring to the boil, reduce the heat, and simmer until very soft. Drain off the stock through a strainer (sieve) and discard.

Put the cooked onion, garlic, and cauliflower into a food processor and blitz to a very smooth purée, adding a drizzle of olive oil if necessary. Taste and adjust the seasoning. If you are using fresh broth, you will need to season properly with salt. If you're using bouillon (stock) cubes you may not need any more salt at all. Keep the purée warm.

Place the chard stalks in a large pan of boiling salted water. Cook until just tender, but not limp. This should take 3–4 minutes, depending on the thickness of the chard—taste a small piece to check. Remove, drain, and season with a pinch of sea salt and a drizzle of olive oil. Boil the chard leaves in the same way, but remove after 2 minutes, drain well, and season with salt and olive oil. Keep warm.

Place two non-stick skillets over a medium-high heat. Drizzle a little olive oil over the sea bass fillets, just enough to coat both sides, and season with salt and pepper. When the pans are hot, place two fillets in each one, skin side down. Fry for 3 minutes without moving, then turn the fish over and fry for 2 minutes more.

Mix the chopped parsley and remaining crushed garlic with a pinch of sea salt and enough olive oil to create a loose parsley oil.

Spoon some of the cauliflower purée onto a plate and place a sea bass fillet on top with the chard twisted over the fish. Drizzle with parsley oil and serve.

Stimulating Spinach Kofta Curry

Indian food incorporates traditional healing herbs and spices that warm the body and the soul. Use a brain-friendly vegetable oil such as olive oil, and avoid common processed vegetable oils. Chili, ginger, cumin, and garlic are flavorful anti-inflammatory ingredients that will make this meal a winner in your home.

For the koftas, sift the gram (chickpea) flour into a large bowl, then gradually stir in ½ cup (120 ml) water to make a very thick batter with no lumps. Add the rest of the ingredients to the batter and stir very well to combine. It should be thick, and the spinach should be bound together by the batter—if it is too dry, add a little water; if it's too wet, add a little flour.

Add ⅜ in. (1 cm) of vegetable oil to a large skillet (frying pan) over a medium heat. When hot, place heaped tablespoons of the batter into the oil, using two spoons to shape it into mounds. Cook in batches for 7–8 minutes, turning a few times, until the koftas are a deep golden brown. Remove with a slotted spoon and drain on paper towels (kitchen paper).

To make the curry, place the tomatoes, chiles, garlic, ginger, onion, and cashew nuts in a food processor and blitz for a few minutes until smooth. Pour the oil into a large skillet over a medium heat. Once hot, add the cumin seeds, ground turmeric, and ground coriander and fry for about 30 seconds. Add the nut paste from the food processor, with the chili powder, garam masala, and salt, and stir well to combine. Turn the heat down to low and cook for about 5 minutes, stirring regularly, until the oil begins to separate from the mixture.

Add 1⅔ cups (400 ml) water and bring to the boil, then turn the heat right down and simmer for 5 minutes. Increase the heat to medium-low, add the koftas, and simmer for about 4 minutes, until they have absorbed some of the water and the curry has thickened. Stir in most of the cilantro (coriander). Serve the curry in bowls, sprinkled with the remaining cilantro, and with the rice on the side.

For the koftas

1¾ cups (220 g) gram (chickpea) flour

8 oz. (250 g) spinach, stems removed, leaves roughly chopped

1 teaspoon ground coriander

¼ teaspoon red chili powder

½-in. (1.25-cm) piece of fresh root ginger, peeled and finely grated

1 fresh green chile, deseeded and finely chopped

1 medium onion, finely chopped

1 garlic clove, crushed

a pinch of baking powder

¾ teaspoon sea salt

For the curry

2 large tomatoes

2 fresh green chiles, deseeded

4 garlic cloves, peeled

1-in. (2.5-cm) piece of fresh root ginger, grated

1 medium onion, peeled and halved

3 tablespoons cashew nuts

3 tablespoons vegetable oil

¼ teaspoon cumin seeds

½ teaspoon ground turmeric

2 teaspoons ground coriander

½ teaspoon red chili powder

½ teaspoon garam masala

1 teaspoon sea salt

a handful of chopped cilantro (coriander) leaves

vegetable oil, for frying

steamed rice, to serve

Serves 4–6

Probiotic Vegan Delight: Greek Salad with Tofu Feta

This is a stand-alone vegetarian dish for a summer night—or you can add a side of animal or fish protein. The fermentation of soy deactivates phytic acid, which adversely affects our thyroid. Besides the many vitamins in this dinner salad, miso and fermented soy are a good source of vitamin K. You'll need to prepare the fermented tofu a day in advance.

For the fermented tofu

about 14 oz. (400 g) plain, extra-firm tofu

1 ⅓ cups (300 g) barley or rice miso

For the salad

2 ripe medium tomatoes

1 green bell pepper, washed and deseeded

1 medium cucumber

⅔ cup (100 g) ripe cherry tomatoes

1 medium red onion, peeled

½ cup (20 g) fresh basil leaves

½ cup (90 g) oven-dried black olives, pitted (stoned)

1 teaspoon dried Mediterranean herbs, plus extra for sprinkling

4 tablespoons extra-virgin olive oil, plus extra for drizzling

sea salt and freshly ground black pepper, to taste

apple cider vinegar, to taste

Serves 4

Slice the block of tofu lengthwise into four equal slices. Spread ⅓ cup (75 g) miso over each slice, covering it entirely. Place the tofu slices in a glass container, cover, and leave to sit at room temperature for 24 hours. The tofu will absorb the saltiness and taste of the miso paste. Scrape off the miso (save it to make soup) and rinse the tofu quickly under running water, if necessary. That's all there is to it!

For the salad, cut the tomatoes and bell pepper into large rounds. Cut the cucumber in half lengthwise and then slice into wedges, leaving the skin on. Cut the cherry tomatoes in half, and chop the onion into thin half-moons. Roughly chop the basil, leaving a couple of leaves whole, for decoration. Put all the vegetables into a large salad bowl, and add the basil, olives, dried herbs, olive oil, a pinch of salt, black pepper, and vinegar, to taste. Quickly toss the ingredients together, preferably with your hands.

To serve, divide the salad among four small plates or shallow bowls, top with the fermented tofu cubes, and finish with a sprinkling of dried herbs and a drizzle of olive oil. Garnish with the reserved basil leaves and enjoy immediately!

TIP: I often ferment tofu in advance and pack it into jars, covered in olive oil, adding Mediterranean herbs, garlic, olives, dried tomatoes, and chili for extra flavor. It keeps this way in the refrigerator for a month, and you can use it to make vegan Greek salad, or serve it as an appetizer.

Broiled Anti-inflammatory Salmon with Leeks and Parmesan

Leeks are underrated; they got left behind with the kale revolution. Yet they are part of the allium family, which is associated with antimicrobial and anti-cancer properties, besides getting rid of uric acid. Yes, leeks are not "sexy," but the sauce, Parmesan cheese, and wild salmon in this dish allow them to shine.

2 medium leeks

1 tablespoon olive oil

½ cup (125 ml) dry white wine

¾ rounded cup (200 ml) crème fraîche

4 tablespoons salted butter

4 fresh salmon fillets

grated Parmesan cheese, for sprinkling

sea salt and freshly ground black pepper

minty green salad, to serve

Serves 4

POWER UP YOUR BRAIN
Leeks, garlic, onions, and scallions all have a long-term anti-aging benefit for cognitive function. (Note that some individuals do not tolerate vegetables of the allium family, especially garlic.) The allium foods shine for their antimicrobial power and ability to lower blood pressure and improve circulation in the brain.

Preheat the broiler (grill) to maximum.

Wash the leeks well, dry them, and cut them into small chunks. Heat the oil in a skillet (frying pan) and sweat the leeks gently, but do not let them brown. When soft, add the wine to the pan to deglaze (dilute and thin) the cooking juices, then add the crème fraîche to make the sauce, and keep warm.

Rub 1 tablespoon of butter into both sides of each piece of salmon, season, and cook on a griddle until just brown and crisp on both sides. Cover with the sauce, sprinkle with Parmesan, and broil (grill) until the cheese is brown and bubbling.

Serve hot from the broiler, accompanied by a minty green salad.

Zesty Carrot and Fennel Soup with Fresh Lemon

This flavorful, versatile French summer soup refreshes the mind and the heart. Garlic boosts the brain, while fennel soothes an irritated gut. For a higher-protein meal, add a side of sliced sausage or free-range chicken breast.

Heat the olive oil in a large pan and add the onion, garlic, carrots, and squash. Toss over a high heat until all the vegetables are beginning to soften at the edges. Add the fennel and broth (stock) and simmer for about 20 minutes until the vegetables are tender. Remove the pan from the heat and stir in the fresh dill, then whizz the soup with a stick blender until very smooth. Stir in the crème fraîche or yogurt and the lemon zest and juice, then sprinkle in the nigella seeds and season to taste.

Serve the soup hot or cold with a sprinkling of chopped black olives and nigella seeds, and a drizzle of extra-virgin olive oil, just enough to leave a glistening trail on top of the soup.

TIP: I love to serve this sunny soup with a side dish of chargrilled Provençal vegetable bruschetta. I use the French bread from the day before and bake it for about 7–10 minutes in a cool oven—about 275°F/140°C/Gas 1—drizzled with olive oil and sprinkled with sea salt. On an open fire (if you have one), barbecue, or chargrill, cook thin slices of eggplant (aubergine), bell peppers, red onion, and zucchini (courgette). Layer the vegetables on the baked bruschetta and stack with sun-blushed tomatoes, black olives, and fresh basil.

2 tablespoons extra-virgin olive oil, plus extra for drizzling

1 onion, diced

2 garlic cloves, crushed

4 carrots, peeled and diced

½ butternut (or other bright-fleshed) squash, peeled, deseeded, and diced

½ fennel bulb, roughly chopped

3⅓ cups (800 ml) vegetable broth (stock)

a small bunch of fresh dill, roughly chopped

½ cup (120 ml) crème fraîche or plain yogurt

grated zest and juice of 1 lemon

½ teaspoon nigella seeds, plus a few extra to garnish

sea salt and freshly ground black pepper

a few very good black olives, finely chopped, to garnish

Serves 4–6

Robust Lamb, Olive, and Feta Burgers

This truly Mediterranean-style burger is perfect for a casual summer dinner, and will satisfy the brain with an abundance of healthy fats. Slow-cook on the grill or in a skillet (frying pan) to preserve vitamin B6, which is easily destroyed by high heat.

1 lb. 2 oz. (500 g) ground (minced) lamb

4 tablespoons (60 g) dried breadcrumbs

1 egg, beaten

½ cup (50 g) pitted (stoned) black olives, chopped

2 oz. (50 g) feta cheese, crumbled

2 tablespoons (30 g) tomato paste (purée)

a large pinch of chopped fresh parsley

1 garlic clove, finely chopped

2 teaspoons olive oil, plus extra for frying

salt and freshly ground black pepper

4 pitas, shredded romaine lettuce, sour cream, and lemon wedges, to serve

Serves 4

Mix all the ingredients, apart from those to serve, thoroughly in a bowl, squeezing the mixture together to help it to bind.

Split the mixture in half, and then in half again, to make four evenly sized burger patties. Flatten them down and try to make them as evenly thick as possible.

Heat a little olive oil in a skillet (frying pan) over a high heat, add the burgers, and fry for 30 seconds on each side. Turn the heat down to medium and fry for another 5 minutes on each side.

These burgers are delicious served in pitas, with shredded romaine lettuce, sour cream, and a squeeze of fresh lemon juice. Season with salt and pepper to taste.

Lamb and Rosemary Meatballs

This is a fragrant and heartwarming dish for any family gathering. Rosemary is rich in phytonutrients and improves memory and blood flow in the brain, as well as warding off infection. For a gluten-free option, experiment with cooked quinoa instead of breadcrumbs, and be creative with lentil or chickpea pasta.

14 oz. (400 g) ground (minced) lamb

2 tablespoons (30 g) dried breadcrumbs

2 tablespoons (30 g) tomato paste (purée)

a pinch of chopped fresh rosemary, or ½ teaspoon dried rosemary

1 garlic clove, very finely chopped

½ teaspoon mustard powder

4 teaspoons (20 g) butter

sea salt and freshly ground black pepper

cooked pasta, to serve

For the sauce (optional)

5 tablespoons (75 ml) white wine

scant 1 cup (200 ml) crème fraîche or sour cream

a large pinch of chopped fresh parsley

Makes 16 meatballs

Mix the lamb, breadcrumbs, tomato paste (purée), rosemary, garlic, mustard powder, salt, and pepper well in a bowl. Divide the mixture into 16 meatballs—the easiest way to make these even is to shape the mixture into a ball, halve it, halve each of those, then again and again, until you have 16 meatballs. It's easier to halve pieces by sight and feel than to take off a meatball piece at a time.

To cook the meatballs, put the butter in a skillet (frying pan) and fry over a medium-high heat for 10–12 minutes until browned and cooked through.

If you wish to make the sauce, add the wine to the skillet once the meatballs are cooked. Bring to the boil, then add the remaining sauce ingredients and season with salt and pepper.

Serve the meatballs and sauce, if using, with pasta.

SUPERFOOD: DAIRY PRODUCTS

Foods such as cream, cheese, butter, yogurt, and kefir have been part of traditional diets for centuries. The saturated fat in full-fat dairy provides building blocks for healthy cell membranes, energy for the brain, and a variety of hormones. Choose whole-fat dairy products that satisfy our brain with their natural taste and texture, and heal our body with fat-soluble vitamins A, D, E, and K.

SIDES
AND
SNACKS

Sharpen Up with Sardine Crostini

Sardines are another top brain food, with high levels of vitamin B12, selenium, protein, and omega-3 oils. Their bones contain a rich source of calcium, which is vital for our memory and nerve cell communication in the brain. Another benefit is that, being small, these wild fish are lower than larger fish in neurotoxic mercury.

4 slices of crusty white bread

1 garlic clove, peeled and cut in half

8 whole sardines (about 3½ oz./100 g each), scaled, gutted, and heads and tails discarded

2 brown onions, sliced into rings

4 tomatoes, diced into ¼-in. (5-mm) pieces

salt and freshly ground black pepper

a small bunch of fresh basil, to serve

Makes 4

Toast the bread under a medium broiler (grill) until lightly golden on both sides. Rub the cut sides of the garlic over each slice of toast. This will give a hint of garlic to the finished crostini, but it won't overpower the other flavors in the dish.

Heat a skillet (frying pan) over a medium heat. Put the sardines in the dry pan and cook for about 10 minutes, turning the fish every minute or so, until they are cooked through and slightly blackened.

Take the pan off the heat and immediately add the onions. After 30 seconds, add the tomatoes. There should be enough residual heat in the pan to heat the tomatoes through but not overcook them.

Place 2 sardines on each slice of toast, and cover with a few spoonfuls of the tomato and onion mixture. Season and garnish with basil leaves before serving.

Blood-sugar Stabilizing Chinese Cabbage Rolls

These cabbage rolls are a perfect—and very nutritious—party snack, or enjoy them as a light lunch with chopsticks. Iodine-rich seaweed provides essential trace minerals for the thyroid. The sauce is rich in fermented foods, including miso, tamari, and apple cider vinegar.

10 Chinese cabbage leaves

3 strips of dried wakame seaweed

10 romaine lettuce leaves

10 red-leaf lettuce leaves

10 long, thin carrot matchsticks

10 thin strips of yellow bell pepper

10 thin strips of red bell pepper

1 tablespoon poppy seeds

sea salt

For the sauce

4 tablespoons almond butter

2 tablespoons white miso or 1 tablespoon dark miso paste (unpasteurized)

apple cider vinegar and tamari soy sauce, to taste

bamboo sushi mat

Serves 2

Put the Chinese cabbage leaves in a shallow bowl, cover with warm water, add a few pinches of salt, and leave to soak for 15 minutes. Soak the wakame seaweed in cold water for 10 minutes.

Drain the Chinese cabbage and pat dry with paper towels (kitchen paper). Drain the soaked wakame and cut each strip lengthwise into four narrower strips.

For the sauce, put all the ingredients in a bowl and mix well, adding a little warm water if needed. The sauce should be quite salty, because only a small amount will be spread inside each roll, so feel free to season generously.

Lay the sushi mat in front of you with the slats running horizontally. Place a cabbage leaf lengthwise on the mat and top with one leaf of each lettuce. Spoon a line of the sauce widthwise along the bottom of the top leaf. Place one strip of carrot, each bell pepper, and wakame along the sauce. You're now ready to roll!

Start rolling from the bottom edge, pushing slightly downward with the mat to create a compact roll. Repeat the whole process with the remaining ingredients.

Wrap the rolls tightly in plastic wrap (cling film) and refrigerate for at least 20 minutes. Cut into 1¼-in. (3-cm) pieces using a wet, sharp knife. Sprinkle with poppy seeds before serving.

POWER UP YOUR BRAIN
Almond butter is rich in vitamin E, protein, antioxidants, and dietary fiber and contributes
to better blood-sugar balance and concentration. Choose unsweetened organic almond
butter to reduce the risk of exposure to mold toxins (that contribute to brain fog), which
are associated with commercial nut butters or bags of nuts.

2 large parsnips, peeled and cubed

1 cucumber, diced

3 large tomatoes, seeded and diced

2 large handfuls of fresh parsley, finely chopped

1 small handful of fresh mint, finely chopped

freshly squeezed juice of 1½ lemons

3 tablespoons olive oil

salt and freshly ground black pepper

Serves 4

Parsnip "Tabbouleh"

Add a Middle Eastern flavor to your repertoire to "internationalize" your taste buds. This dish is loaded with health-boosting vitamins C, E, and K and potassium. It is also a great source of folate, which our brain needs and our heart loves. In this gluten-free version, peeled and cubed parsnip replaces the more usual bulgur wheat, giving a refreshing taste for any party plate.

Put the parsnips in a food processor and pulse a few times until finely chopped to resemble grains of bulgur wheat. Transfer to a bowl.

Add the cucumber, tomatoes, parsley, and mint to the bowl, and stir everything together. Add the lemon juice, olive oil, and salt and pepper, to taste. Mix well.

Leave the salad in the refrigerator for at least an hour before serving, or overnight if possible, to allow the flavors to develop.

Turmeric and Chile Kimchee

Kimchee is a staple of Korean cuisine, and is now gaining popularity in the West as a tasty condiment. Fermented foods are traditional, and this kimchee is chock-full of anti-inflammatory turmeric, ginger, and garlic, which promote microcirculation in the brain. (Leave out the chile if you can't tolerate hot spices.)

3 tablespoons (60 g) sea salt

6 cups (1.2 liters) cold water

7 cups (600 g) green cabbage, cut into thick strips

8 carrots (about 1 lb. 3 oz./520 g total weight), cut into bite-sized pieces

¾-oz. (20-g) piece of fresh root ginger

4 garlic cloves

4 small whole red chiles

1 teaspoon ground turmeric

½ teaspoon chili powder

pickle press (optional)

Makes 3–4 cups (300–400 g)

Make a brine by stirring the salt into the water.

Put the cabbage and carrots into the pickle press (if using), and cover with the brine. Screw the lid down a little, to keep the vegetables submerged. If you don't have a pickle press, put the vegetables and brine into a bowl and weigh them down by resting a plate on top of them. Leave the cabbage and carrots to soak for a few hours or overnight.

When the soaking time is up, drain the vegetables, reserving the brine. Chop the ginger and garlic and add to the vegetables with the chiles and ground spices.

Put the mixture back into the pickle press or bowl and add enough brine to rise over the vegetables once you press them down. Screw the lid down as far as you can, or, if using a plate, put something heavy on top of it to weigh it down. The vegetables must be submerged in the brine throughout the fermentation process. Check every 2 days and remove any foam or mold spots that appear on the surface, which is totally normal. Allow to ferment for a minimum of 1 week; the best taste develops after 4 weeks. When the vegetables are ready, transfer them to sterilized jars (see page 9), cover with the brine, and keep in the refrigerator.

Brain Power Bites

These beautiful canapes will create a lot of chatter around your summer party platter. Watermelon is a terrific source of potassium, which balances sodium in the diet. If you get cramps or heart palpitations, low potassium could be the reason (and low magnesium, too). Meanwhile, the Artichoke, Mozzarella, and Speck canapes are protein-packed, quick and easy to make, and a good blood-sugar stabilizer to boot. The artichoke is often said to be a vegetable, but it is actually a member of the thistle family. Its benefits include aiding in digestive troubles, lowering blood pressure, and protecting against heart disease and stroke. What a refreshing assortment of tastes in these delicious snacks!

Watermelon, Feta, Basil, and Balsamic

1 watermelon, cubed

3½ oz. (100 g) feta cheese, cut into 40 pieces

40 small basil leaves

3 tablespoons balsamic reduction

Makes 40

Cut the watermelon into 1-in. (2.5-cm) cubes and spoon out a little hole at the top of each cube, for stuffing with cheese later. Place the cubes upside down on paper towels (kitchen paper) and leave for 30 minutes in the refrigerator. Check after 15 minutes and replace the paper towels (kitchen paper) if they are wet through.

Take the watermelon out of the refrigerator and place the cubes hole-side up on a serving board or platter. Place a piece of feta in the hole, put a small basil leaf (upside down) on top, and drizzle in a little balsamic reduction. Serve.

Artichoke, Mozzarella, and Speck

5 slices of speck or serrano ham (about 2½ oz./70 g)

4½-oz. (125-g) ball of buffalo mozzarella

15 chargrilled artichoke heart quarters, from a jar

15 small basil leaves

freshly ground black pepper

Makes 15

Cut each slice of speck or serrano ham crosswise into three pieces, to make 15 pieces in total. Slice the mozzarella into 15 even pieces.

Drain the artichoke heart quarters in a strainer (sieve), then place them on paper towels (kitchen paper) to remove any excess oil.

Place a piece of speck on a board and put an artichoke quarter, a slice of mozzarella, and a basil leaf on top. Sprinkle with ground black pepper, then roll the ham around the filling. Repeat with the remaining ingredients. Serve.

Great-for-the-Gut Skewers

Here are two fantastic party skewer recipes. Spicy shrimp (prawns) and luscious mango on a stick (below): what a great combination for a party platter! Fresh mangoes are rich in fiber, quercitin (a natural antihistamine), and plant enzymes that aid digestion, ease pain, and heal wounds. No wonder mango is known as "king of the fruits." Opposite, the flavorful jerk chicken with culinary and medicinal spices is a tasty party snack. With the microbiome being a trendy "foodie" topic, it certainly hits the mark on prebiotics, too. Plantain is rich in soluble fiber (prebiotics), which feeds the health-promoting microbes in our gut.

Jamaican-spiced Prawn and Mango Skewers

For the curry powder

1 teaspoon fennel seeds

1 teaspoon fenugreek seeds

1 teaspoon mustard seeds

2 tablespoons coriander seeds

1 tablespoon cumin seeds

1 teaspoon ground allspice

2 tablespoons ground turmeric

6 oz. (170 g) raw, shelled shrimp (prawns)

sunflower oil

1 mango

a handful of fresh cilantro (coriander)

freshly squeezed juice of 1 lime

spice grinder or pestle and mortar

25 mini wooden skewers

Makes 25

NOTE: This makes four times the curry powder you will need, so if you are making more than 25 skewers, there is no need to multiply the curry powder.

To make the curry powder, put all the spices except the allspice and turmeric in a dry skillet (frying pan), and cook over a medium heat for a few minutes, until fragrant but not darkened.

Leave to cool, then transfer to a spice grinder or pestle and mortar. Grind thoroughly, then stir in the allspice and turmeric.

Sprinkle the shrimp (prawns) with 1 heaped teaspoon of the curry powder and a little sunflower oil. Mix and leave to marinate in the refrigerator for at least 2 hours.

Slice the mango into 1-in. (2.5-cm) squares, ¼ in. (6 mm) deep.

Heat 1 tablespoon sunflower oil in a skillet, add the shrimp, and sauté for a few minutes, until cooked through.

Place a cilantro (coriander) leaf on top of each mango cube and sprinkle with a little lime juice. Top each with a shrimp, and skewer.

Jerk Chicken and Plantain Skewers

For the marinade

1 tablespoon freshly chopped thyme leaves

1 Scotch bonnet chile, deseeded (or 2 red chiles, seeds left in)

5 scallions (spring onions), roughly chopped

1 teaspoon salt

1 tablespoon soy sauce

3 large garlic cloves

thumb-sized piece of fresh root ginger, grated

2 tablespoons white wine vinegar

1 tablespoon soft light brown sugar

1 teaspoon ground allspice

1 teaspoon freshly ground black pepper

1 teaspoon ground cinnamon

½ teaspoon freshly grated nutmeg

1 lb. 2 oz. (500 g) boneless, skinless chicken thighs

2 ripe plantains

2 tablespoons sunflower oil

36 mini wooden skewers

Makes 36

Whizz all the marinade ingredients in a food processor until smooth.

Cut each chicken thigh into six pieces, place in a bowl, and pour the marinade over. Cover and refrigerate for at least 6 hours, or overnight.

Cut the plantains lengthwise down the middle, then into ½-in. (1-cm) pieces.

When you are almost ready to serve, cook the chicken pieces on a very hot griddle for a few minutes on each side, until cooked through. Transfer to a warm plate.

Heat the oil in a skillet (frying pan). Sauté the plantain in two batches for 2 minutes on each side.

Skewer the chicken and plantain (as shown below) and serve.

Brain-healthy Chips

Variety is the spice of life! And so it is with food. Be creative and integrate a kaleidoscope of different foods that contain polyphenols, carotenoids, organosulfides, phenols, flavonoids, and so on. Let's just call them a medley of craveable chips (crisps) that will spruce up any protein dish on your plate.

Curried Sweet Potato

2 medium sweet potatoes

5 tablespoons coconut oil

1 tablespoon curry powder

1 or 2 baking sheets, greased and lined with baking parchment

Serves 4

Preheat the oven to 400°F/200°C/Gas 6.

Slice the sweet potatoes into thin rounds using a vegetable peeler or mandoline, and place them in a large, shallow dish.

Warm the coconut oil in a small pan over a low heat, until liquefied. Remove from the heat and stir in the curry powder. Pour the heated mixture over the sweet potato rounds, toss carefully to coat the vegetable slices, then place the rounds on the prepared baking sheet(s).

Bake for 22 minutes, or until completely crisp, checking them halfway through and turning them over if necessary. Remove from the oven and serve in bowls.

Brussels Sprouts

4 cups (400 g) Brussels sprouts

1 tablespoon olive oil (or freshly squeezed lime juice)

½ tablespoon ground cumin

½ teaspoon salt

1 or 2 baking sheets, greased and lined with baking parchment

Serves 4

Preheat the oven to 350°F/180°C/Gas 4.

Using a sharp knife, carefully slice off the very bottom of the Brussels sprouts to render the leaves loose. Remove as many leaves as you can into a mixing bowl, and discard the cores.

Toss the leaves with the olive oil, cumin, and salt. For an oil-free option, substitute the olive oil for lime juice.

Arrange the leaves on the prepared baking sheet(s) and bake for 10–12 minutes until the leaves are dry and crispy. Remove from the oven and serve in bowls.

Beet

2 beets (beetroot), peeled

1 golden beet, peeled

1 tablespoon olive oil

sea salt

1 or 2 baking sheets, greased and lined with baking parchment

Serves 4

Preheat the oven to 350°F/180°C/Gas 4.

Using a sharp knife, thinly slice off the very bottoms and tops of all the beets (beetroot). Thinly slice the trimmed beets into rounds using a vegetable peeler or a mandoline, and place them in a large, shallow dish.

Toss them in the olive oil to coat, transfer the beet slices to the prepared baking sheet(s), and bake for 20–22 minutes, or until crispy.

Remove from the oven and place on paper towels (kitchen paper) to remove any excess oil. Sprinkle with sea salt and serve.

Gut–Brain Juggernaut Purple Sauerkraut with Dulse and Caraway Seeds

Sauerkraut, a traditional German fermented cabbage, is a versatile and colorful addition to the food plate. Consider it for a delicious topping or garnish on a summer sandwich, or add it as a side dish to your grilled chicken breast or fish fillet. It also adds color and crunch when added to a summer salad or the traditional barbecue hotdog. Sauerkraut is also a terrific gut-friendly fermented food, rich in vitamin C and enzymes.

1½ teaspoons caraway seeds

½ oz. (10 g) dulse seaweed

1 medium red cabbage (about 1¾ lb./800 g)

2½ teaspoons salt

pickle press, clean glass jar, or crock

Makes 2 cups (200 g)

Use a pestle and mortar to crush the caraway seeds. Cover the dulse with water and leave to soak for 10 minutes. Very finely chop or grate the cabbage.

Add the salt to the cabbage and squeeze with clean hands to release the juices. Add the drained and chopped seaweed and crushed caraway seeds. The cabbage should be dripping wet.

To ensure proper fermentation without the presence of oxygen, carefully pack the cabbage and its juice into a pickle press, large jar, or crock. It should always be submerged in its own brine, so stuff it tightly and screw down the lid of the pickle press as much as you can. If using a jar or crock, pack the cabbage in tightly, cover with a plate that fits inside, and place a weight on top (such as a glass bottle filled with water, a marble weight, or a stone).

Check after 12 hours and press again; the cabbage will wilt farther and more juice will come out. The shortest time for fermentation to take place is 3 days, but I usually leave it for at least 7 days, and ideally for 4 weeks. During this time, it's necessary to check your press, jar, or crock every other day and remove any foam and/or mold that forms on the surface of the brine—this is quite normal and will not affect the quality of your sauerkraut in any way.

After up to 4 weeks, transfer the sauerkraut to sterilized jars (see page 9), cover in the brine, and refrigerate. It will stay fresh for at least a month, and possibly 2–3 months. Bring it to room temperature before eating to ensure that you're taking in the maximum amount of good bacteria.

SUPERFOOD: SAUERKRAUT

Besides providing easy-to-absorb nutrients, sauerkraut is high in fiber, which lowers blood sugar and enhances bowel activity. Fermented foods fortify the immune function of our gut (although they can be contraindicated for those with high histamine levels).

Zen with Tahini, Lemon and Parsley Dip

This is one of my favorites, and always a hit at parties. Tahini is loaded with vitamin E, rich in linoleic acid, which protects our gut and brain membranes, and contains mood-enhancing amino acids. This smooth dip is inviting with sliced carrots, celery, bell peppers, or cucumbers. Yummy.

½ cup (150 g) plus 2 tablespoons light or dark tahini

freshly squeezed juice of 2 lemons

2 garlic cloves, crushed

a small bunch of fresh flat-leaf parsley, finely chopped

1–2 tablespoons pomegranate seeds

sea salt and freshly ground black pepper

warm bread, or thinly sliced carrot, celery, or bell pepper, to serve

Serves 4

In a bowl, beat the tahini until smooth. Gradually beat in the lemon juice—the mixture will thicken at first and then loosen—and add several teaspoons of cold water to lighten the mixture until it is the consistency of heavy (double) cream.

Add the garlic and season well with salt and pepper. Stir in most of the parsley, spoon the mixture into a serving bowl, and garnish with the rest of the parsley and the pomegranate seeds. Serve with warm bread, or with thin strips of celery, carrot, or bell pepper.

Energy-bursting Mini Meatballs

Naturally-raised or grass-fed lamb, an underrated brain food, has always been favored in traditional Middle Eastern and Mediterranean cuisines for its abundance of protein, vitamin B12, selenium, zinc, iron, and phosphorous. Selenium, a trace mineral, is required for optimal thyroid, brain, immune, and detox functions.
This is a tasty party treat for the meat-lover!

2–3 tablespoons pistachios, shelled

9 oz. (250 g) lean ground (minced) lamb

1 onion, finely chopped

2 garlic cloves, crushed

2 teaspoons ground cinnamon

a small bunch of fresh flat-leaf parsley, finely chopped

sunflower oil, for frying

sea salt and freshly ground black pepper

lemon wedges, to serve

Serves 4–6

Roast the pistachios in a small, heavy pan for 1–2 minutes, until they emit a nutty aroma. Using a pestle and mortar, crush them lightly to break them into small pieces.

In a bowl, pound the lamb with the onion, garlic, and cinnamon. Knead the mixture with your hands and slap it down into the base of the bowl to knock out the air. Add the parsley, season, and knead well to make sure it is thoroughly mixed.

Take cherry-size portions of the mixture in your hands and roll them into balls. Indent each ball with your finger, right into the middle, and fill the hollow with a few of the crushed pistachios. Seal it by squeezing the mixture over it and then rolling the ball once more.

Heat a thin layer of oil in a heavy skillet (frying pan). Place the meatballs in the skillet and cook them on all sides, until nicely browned. Drain on paper towels (kitchen paper), sprinkle with the remaining crushed pistachios, and serve with lemon wedges to squeeze over.

SMOOTHIES
AND
ELIXIRS

Green-a-colada to Protect Your Brain

If you enjoy the flavors of the Caribbean, why not try this fruit
and vegetable smoothie anchored with coconut milk? Pineapples
are rich in an enzyme called bromelain, which aids inflammation,
digestion, allergies, and arthritic joints, and reduces the risk of
dementia and Alzheimer's disease. (For lower sugar content,
use only one type of fruit.)

3 cups (400 g) pineapple chunks

1 banana, peeled

2 cups (500 ml) coconut water

3 cups (150 g) spinach (fresh or frozen)

1 tablespoon coconut oil (optional)

2 tablespoons hemp seeds, 2 tablespoons
unsweetened dried shredded (desiccated)
coconut, or sliced fresh pineapple, to serve
(optional)

Serves 2-4

Put the pineapple and banana in separate freezer bags and freeze for
at least 8 hours, or overnight.

Put the coconut water in a blender with the frozen pineapple, frozen
banana, spinach, and coconut oil (if using). Blend until smooth.

Pour the smoothie into two tall glasses or four smaller glasses to serve.
Top each with hemp seeds and shredded (desiccated) coconut if you
wish, or, for added extravagance, put a slice of fresh pineapple on the
rim of each glass.

1 cucumber

5 celery ribs (stalks)

3½ oz. (100 g) broccoli

¼ fennel bulb

½ zucchini (courgette)

1 apple

1 lime, peeled

3 large handfuls of fresh parsley

3 large handfuls of spinach or kale

juicer

Serves 2 or 3

If you are using a masticating juicer, run all the ingredients through the juicer. If you have a centrifugal juicer, alternate leaves with the celery and apple to prevent them from getting caught in the machine.

Divide the juice between 2 or 3 glasses and serve.

Green Brain Energy Juice

This super liver detox drink is loaded with chlorophyll, sulfurphane (an anti-cancer agent) in the broccoli, and anti-inflammatory celery. A vitamin-rich green drink, it is a brain and energy booster. (Do steam, rather than boil, the broccoli, to offset its thyroid-inhibiting properties. If you have joint pain, kidney stones, headaches, or cataracts, leave out the spinach.)

Carrot and Lemon Juice with Omega-3 Oils

Ready for sunshine in a glass? This whole-food vitamin C and beta-carotene booster will liven up any morning. We need these vitamins for our skin, gums, blood vessels, and immune system, and to help remove toxins from our body. Omega-3 oils, such as flaxseed oil, are in dark-colored bottles as they are sensitive to light exposure (and higher temperatures). If you are not sure what to buy, talk to someone at your local health store.

2¾ lb. (1.2 kg) carrots

freshly squeezed juice of 2 lemons

2–4 teaspoons omega-3 oils (such as flaxseed oil, or a combination of flaxseed, primrose, and pumpkin oils), to taste

juicer

Serves 2

Put the carrots in the juicer and blitz until all the juice is extracted. Whisk in the lemon juice and oils to taste until well mixed.

Divide the juice between 2 glasses and serve immediately.

POWER UP YOUR BRAIN
Ongoing exposure to pesticides, plastics, and growth hormones in commercial foods, even if low-grade, alters our moods, lowers our attention span, affects blood-sugar balance, and contributes to infertility. More than ever we need vitamins from foods, especially vitamin C. In addition, flaxseed oil promotes better hormonal balance and moods and lowers inflammation.

Antioxidant-rich Red Smoothie

Tasty, antioxidant-rich rooibos (or redbush) tea has long been a staple in South Africa, where I grew up. It is also oxalate- and caffeine-free, and low in tannins— so it won't stain your teeth!

1¼ cups (300 ml) rooibos tea, cooled

2 medium apples, peeled, cored, and chopped

1 medium beet (beetroot), peeled and chopped

⅝-in. (1.5-cm) piece of fresh root ginger, peeled and finely grated

1–2 teaspoons wheatgrass powder

Serves 2

Put the cooled rooibos tea, apples, and beet (beetroot) in a blender. Squeeze the juice from the grated ginger through your fingers and add to the blender with the wheatgrass powder, then blend until smooth.

Divide the juice between 2 glasses and serve immediately.

Brain Booster

Our brain needs energy all day long. Whether you prefer a morning power-up or an afternoon pick-me-up, this super-nutritious shake will keep your mind sharp and ready to go. It's great for kids and adults alike.

a small handful of goji berries

generous ¾ cup (200 ml) plain bio yogurt

⅔ cup (150 ml) coconut drinking milk

3 Brazil nuts

1 tablespoon hemp protein powder

2 handfuls of blueberries

1 teaspoon blackcurrant powder

1 teaspoon camu camu powder

Serves 2

Soak the goji berries in 4 tablespoons of warm water for 30 minutes, until softened. Put them in a blender with the soaking water and the rest of the ingredients and blend until smooth.

Divide between 2 glasses and serve immediately.

POWER UP YOUR BRAIN
Brazil nuts are the best food source of selenium, a trace mineral that is essential for optimal thyroid and immune function, and a key factor in calming excessive inflammation. Selenium is also implicated in decreasing anxiety and lifting depressed moods. Soak the nuts to remove phytic acid for maximum health benefit.

Trio of Brain Tonics

When I was a kid, my parents insisted that I take a spoonful of herbal tonic every morning before school. Now we have fun tonic drinks that benefit our body and brain. These tonics are low in sugar, but high in electrolytes and anti-inflammatory action. Mix in a teaspoon of flaxseed or hempseed oil to ensure optimal absorption and blood-sugar balance.

Turmeric Tonic

2-in. (5-cm) piece of fresh root ginger, peeled

1 teaspoon ground turmeric

2 teaspoons lemon juice

a pinch of salt

a pinch of freshly ground black pepper

stevia, to taste

1 cup ice cubes

juicer

Serves 1

Extract the juice from the ginger using a juicer (you need about 1 teaspoon). Transfer to a mixing pitcher (jug) or shaker with the remaining ingredients and 1 cup (250 ml) of water. Stir well, pour into a glass, and serve immediately.

Date-orade

1 ½ cups (375 ml) coconut water, chilled

2 fresh dates, pitted (stoned)

a few drops of pure vanilla extract

a pinch of pink Himalayan salt, to taste

Serves 1

Put all the ingredients into a blender and blend until smooth and frothy. Pour into a glass and serve immediately.

Carob Latte

1 ½ cups (375 ml) almond milk

1 tablespoon decaffeinated espresso powder (or Dandy Blend)

1 ½ teaspoons carob powder

a few drops of pure vanilla extract

a pinch of pink Himalayan salt

1 teaspoon clear honey (optional)

juicer

Serves 1

Heat the almond milk gently in a pan over a medium heat. Put the remaining ingredients in a mixing pitcher (jug) or shaker and stir or shake until well combined. Add the warm almond milk and stir or shake again. Pour into a glass and serve immediately.

VARIATION: You can also make an iced latte by mixing all the ingredients in a mixing pitcher or shaker, without warming the almond milk, and adding ½ cup of ice cubes.

Probiotic Smoothies

These homemade probiotic drinks offer many benefits. The Very Pink Yogurt Smoothie is a quick and tasty blood sugar pick-me-up. Cultured foods such as yogurt are a great source of calcium, vitamin D, and probiotics that encourage microbial diversity in the gut. The fiber in the dates is a prebiotic substrate, but for a low-sugar option, use stevia instead of dates. (Dates raise blood sugar, while stevia does not.) Try the Coconut Kefir Smoothie for a terrific thirst-quencher on a summer day. Add brain-friendly coconut milk if you prefer a creamier smoothie version. A sprinkling of sea salt bumps up the electrolytes.

Very Pink Yogurt Smoothie

2 cups (480 ml) yogurt (see page 52)

1 cup (130 g) raspberries or pitted (stoned) sour cherries

2 oz. (60 g) (about 6) Medjool dates, pitted (stoned)

Serves 2

In a high-speed blender, blend all the ingredients until silky smooth. If you're using frozen fruit, thaw in advance. In summer, for a cool and refreshing smoothie, frozen fruits can be blended in directly.

VARIATION: A purple smoothie can be made by substituting blueberries or blackberries for the raspberries or sour cherries, while a green version can be made with one apple and ½ cup (120 ml) green juice (made from kale, chard, spinach, etc.). For a taste of the tropics, blend in mango, pineapple, or papaya.

Coconut Kefir Smoothie

2 tablespoons water kefir grains (see page 54)

2 cups (480 ml) coconut water

1 cup (240 ml) full-fat coconut milk

1 fully ripe mango (approximately 12 oz./340 g) or other ripe and sweet fruit, peeled and cut into large chunks

maple, rice, or agave syrup, to taste (optional)

34-fl. oz. (1-litre) preserving jar with tight-fitting lid

plastic strainer (sieve)

wooden or plastic spoon

Serves 2

Put the water kefir grains in the jar, add the coconut water, and stir well. Cover it loosely or seal with the jar lid (I prefer sealing the jar to get more fizziness). Keep the jar away from direct sunlight and leave to ferment for 2 days, stirring a couple times in those 48 hours. Taste the liquid—it should be more sour than sweet. Strain it into a blender, add the coconut milk and the mango or other fruit, and blend until completely smooth. Taste and add a little maple, rice, or agave syrup as necessary.

VARIATION: This probiotic smoothie can also be made with pineapple, strawberries, or peaches.
In hot weather, add some ice chips before blending.

DESSERTS AND TREATS

Pow-wow Paleo Cookies

In South Africa we dunked cookies into our afternoon tea, and to this day I keep "dunking." These cookies are dense in nutrients, with fatty acids that provide long-lasting energy for the body and brain. Pack a low-carb paleo cookie in your lunchbox, or enjoy it with a cup of tea.

2 teaspoons ground chia seeds (buy them ready ground, or grind whole seeds in a coffee or spice grinder)

2 tablespoons water

about 1½ cups (170 g) pecans (see method), or ground almonds/almond meal

3 tablespoons unsweetened dried shredded (desiccated) coconut

1 teaspoon ground cinnamon

½ teaspoon grated nutmeg

1 teaspoon baking powder

a pinch of salt

a dash of vanilla extract

3 teaspoons stevia

2 tablespoons almond milk

Makes 16 small cookies

Preheat the oven to 350°F/180°C/Gas 4 and line a baking sheet with baking parchment.

Put the ground chia seeds and water in a small bowl. Whisk the seeds into the water with a fork until the mixture is the consistency of a beaten egg—in fact, what you now have is two "chia eggs," which play the same role as eggs in plant-based baking recipes. Place in the refrigerator.

Put the pecans or almonds into a food processor and blitz to a fine powder. You don't want to overprocess them, as they will start to form a paste instead. You should end up with 1 cup of flour—make sure you have this much, and blitz more pecans if you don't. In a bowl, combine the pecan flour, coconut, cinnamon, nutmeg, baking powder, and salt.

Add the "chia eggs," vanilla extract, stevia, and almond milk to the bowl of dry ingredients, and mix well. Divide the mixture into 16 and shape each portion into balls, then flatten them between your palms to make little cookies. Arrange them on the prepared baking sheet.

Bake in the preheated oven for about 6 minutes. Transfer to a wire rack to cool completely, then store in an airtight container for up to 4 days.

SUPERFOOD: DARK CHOCOLATE

Dark chocolate, with its medicinal, mood-enhancing, and aphrodisiac properties, is also known as "food of the gods," and for good reason, too. It boosts endorphins and the bitterness aids digestion. Do buy organic as much of the world's chocolate supply is contaminated with mold toxins (such as peanuts and corn). From a nutrient perspective, it is rich in magnesium and polyphenols that are needed for every biochemical action in the brain. Many do not know that organic chocolate is also a prebiotic that positively affects bifidia bacteria.

Healing Hand-rolled Macaroons

Who doesn't like a treat that packs lots of raw nutrition, too? Choose from the variety of macaroons and see which one you enjoy most. Each one brings a different taste and nutritional benefit to the table. Molasses are rich in iron, honey boosts the immune system, and applesauce is a prebiotic. Macaroons are great for a guilt-free dessert, or a treat with a cup of tea in the afternoon.

Cocoa Coconut

½ cup (40 g) unsweetened dried shredded (desiccated) coconut

¼ cup (30 g) unsweetened cocoa powder, plus extra for rolling

3 tablespoons sugar-free honey

2 teaspoons granulated stevia

3 tablespoons coconut oil

1½ teaspoons pure vanilla extract

Winter Spice

½ cup (40 g) unsweetened dried shredded (desiccated) coconut, plus extra for rolling

¼ cup (30 g) almond meal

4 tablespoons sugar-free blackstrap molasses

1 teaspoon granulated stevia

½ teaspoon grated fresh root or ground ginger

½ teaspoon ground cinnamon

¼ teaspoon ground nutmeg

3 tablespoons coconut oil

Apple and Cinnamon

½ cup (40 g) unsweetened dried shredded (desiccated) coconut, plus extra for rolling

¼ cup (30 g) almond meal

4 tablespoons sugar-free applesauce (apple purée)

¾ teaspoons ground cinnamon

1 teaspoon granulated stevia

1 teaspoon pure vanilla extract

3 tablespoons coconut oil

Each makes 8–10

Each of these macaroons can be made in the same way. Put all the ingredients into a mixing bowl and stir to combine.

Shape the mixture into balls using your hands or a melon baller, arrange on a clean baking sheet and transfer to the refrigerator to chill for at least 20 minutes, or until firm.

Meanwhile, sift a little extra cocoa powder or coconut onto a wide plate and set aside.

Remove the macaroons from the fridge and roll them in the cocoa powder or coconut before serving.

Tantalizing Chocolate and Nut Butter Tart

Planning a celebration at home? This gluten- and dairy-free tart is a showstopper for any occasion. Prebiotics, polyphenols, and unrefined omega-6 and omega-9 fatty acids combine to create a nutrient-dense dessert for chocolate-lovers of any age. Did you know that chocolate is a mood-enhancer—and an aphrodisiac, too?

For the base

½ cup (80 g) pecans

4 oz. (110 g) oatcakes

3 oz. (90 g) dried pitted (stoned) dates

1 tablespoon coconut oil

4 teaspoons unsweetened cocoa powder

1 tablespoon pure maple syrup

a pinch of sea salt

For the nut butter layer

1¼ cups (175 g) pitted Medjool dates

5 tablespoons rice milk

¾ cup (200 g) smooth nut butter

2 tablespoons coconut oil, melted

2 tablespoons pure maple syrup

For the chocolate layer

6½ oz. (200 g) avocado

3 tablespoons unsweetened cocoa powder

4½ tablespoons pure maple syrup

a pinch of sea salt

2 tablespoons coconut oil, melted

3 tablespoons (25 g) whole almonds, roasted

1 tablespoon coconut palm sugar

3½ oz. (100 g) bittersweet (dark) chocolate, sweetened with natural sugar

Serves 10–12

Grease an 8-in. (20-cm) loose-bottomed cake pan (tin) with vegetable oil. Lightly roast the pecans in a separate roasting tray at 350°F/180°C/Gas 4 for 3–4 minutes, or until they are a shade darker and aromatic. Leave to cool. Place all the base ingredients in a food processor and blitz until the mixture sticks together when pressed between your fingers. Press firmly into the cake pan to make a smooth, even base. Leave to set in the refrigerator for 30 minutes, or in the freezer for 15 minutes.

For the nut butter layer, blitz the dates and rice milk to a smooth paste in a food processor. Add the nut butter and blitz for a couple seconds until just combined. Pour in the coconut oil and maple syrup and blitz for another few seconds until incorporated. Don't blitz for any longer, or the coconut oil will split away from the oil in the nuts. Maple syrup also causes nut butter to seize and become thicker, so don't worry if the mixture becomes firm. Spread it over the base in the cake pan and level with the back of a spoon dipped in boiling water. Cover and place in the refrigerator or freezer while you make the chocolate layer.

To make the chocolate layer, add the avocado, cocoa powder, maple syrup, and salt to a food processor. Blitz until smooth, then pour in the melted coconut oil and blitz briefly to combine. Spoon it over the chocolate mixture in the cake pan and level out. Return it to the refrigerator or freezer.

Place the roasted almonds in a dry skillet (frying pan) with 1 tablespoon coconut palm sugar, and heat through until the sugar melts and coats the nuts. Leave to cool and chop roughly.

Make chocolate curls by melting the chocolate and spreading it out in a thin layer on a large, flat baking sheet. Put aside until just set, but not solid, and check it regularly—it is important that it does not set completely. Using a flat-edged spatula, scrape the chocolate from the baking sheet, pushing away from you. (You can use a hairdryer to get it back to the right consistency if it is too firmly set.) Place the curls in the fridge to set and then tumble them onto the tart with the almonds. Keep the tart in the freezer and remove it 30–45 minutes before serving.

Happy-mood Truffles with Dates, Pistachios, Coconut, and Honey

This is a real treat for the sweet-lover. Dates are high in sugar, but they are also high in fiber and aid the digestive process. They are potassium-rich sweet treats that aid the alertness and speed of brain activity. (If you have type 2 diabetes or problems with blood sugar and insulin resistance, avoid high-sugar treats.)

2 scant cups (250 g) shelled, unsalted pistachios

2 scant cups (250 g) pitted (stoned) dates, roughly chopped

2 teaspoons ground cinnamon

2 teaspoons rosewater

1 tablespoon runny honey

3 tablespoons unsweetened dried shredded (desiccated) coconut

Serves 6–8

Dry-roast the pistachios in a small, heavy skillet (frying pan) until they emit a nutty aroma. Using a pestle and mortar or a blender, grind them coarsely.

Add the dates and cinnamon and pound, or blend them with the ground pistachios to form a thick paste. Drizzle in the rosewater and honey while you are doing this to help loosen the mixture, although it will become stickier.

Once the paste is fairly smooth, dampen your fingers and mold small portions into cherry-sized balls. Spread out the coconut on a plate and roll the little truffles in it, making sure they are evenly coated.

Pop the truffles into a sealed container and keep in the refrigerator until you are ready to use them. They can be served chilled or at room temperature, and go well with salty and spicy mezze dishes. The truffles will keep for 2–3 weeks in the refrigerator.

POWER UP YOUR BRAIN

Pistachios, which grow on small bushy trees widely located in regions of Central Asia and the Middle East, have been used for centuries in sweet dishes, delicacies, and massage oils. The nuts are rich in protein, vitamins E, B6 (especially gamma-tocopherol), and A, and heart-healthy monounsaturated fats (known as oleic acid). All support the heart, eyes, and nervous system. It is best to buy unshelled nuts instead of salted and sweetened pistachios. Store them in a container in the fridge to prevent them from turning rancid.

1 cup (170–180 g) basmati rice

2½ cups (600 ml) low-fat or whole milk

14-oz (400-g) can coconut milk

1 teaspoon vanilla extract

½ cup (100 g) granulated sugar

seeds from 5 cardamom pods, crushed to a fine powder with a pestle and mortar

Serves 4

Place all the ingredients into a large pan. Bring to the boil, then simmer for 20 minutes until creamy. Serve immediately.

If (for some odd reason) you don't eat it all, keep the rice pudding in the refrigerator. It will become very solid, but you can add a little milk or cream to loosen it up before eating.

Nourishing Rice Pudding with Cardamom

We all need a treat sometimes—so why not make it a healthy one? Creamy coconut milk is a favorite of mine, as it nourishes the brain, thyroid, and immune system, while also curbing food cravings. Instead of sugar, you could try some raw honey, and perhaps add a small sprinkling of sea salt.

Low-sugar Chocolate Mousse

Ready for decadence? Dark chocolate mousse is a favorite for many—and this one is gluten- and dairy-free, too. Smooth with a sweet-bitter overtone, creamy with coconut milk and avocado, and with a drizzle of aromatic rosemary caramel, it will create a big finish. Beware that oxalates in chocolate and histamine in avocado are associated with headaches, though.

Melt the coconut oil in a heatproof bowl set over a pan of simmering water.

Add the flesh of the avocados, cocoa powder, maple syrup, vanilla, and a good pinch of sea salt to a food processor and blitz for a few seconds. Add the melted coconut oil and blitz until completely smooth. Remove to a bowl, cover, and refrigerate for at least 2 hours.

To make the caramel, place the coconut milk and coconut palm sugar in a pan over a medium-high heat. Bring to the boil, stirring all the time, then reduce the heat, add the rosemary and a pinch of sea salt, and simmer for 10 minutes, stirring on and off, until you have a thick, viscous caramel.

When ready to serve, warm the caramel, then spoon the chocolate mousse onto four cold bowls or plates. Drizzle over the warm rosemary caramel, add a few raspberries to each dish and sprinkle over some rosemary leaves and a very small pinch of sea salt. Serve immediately.

3 tablespoons coconut oil

2 large ripe avocados

¼ cup (4 tablespoons) unsweetened cocoa powder

¼ cup (4 tablespoons) pure maple syrup

1 teaspoon pure vanilla extract

¾ cup (200 ml) coconut milk

½ cup (100 g) coconut palm sugar

2 sprigs of rosemary, plus a few leaves to serve

about 15 raspberries

sea salt

Serves 4

Performance-boosting Breakfast Bars

These yummy bars can be a great snack when you are on the go, or an afternoon treat with a cup of tea. Raisins provide natural sweetness, while the seeds are a great source of the unrefined omega-6 fatty acids our body needs. Be creative and try different ingredients, such as hazelnut butter instead of tahini, prunes or dried cranberries in place of raisins, and orange juice (and zest) instead of lemon. You could also use soaked steel-cut oats instead of old-fashioned oats, for a chewier texture.

2 small bananas, peeled

2 cups (180 g) old-fashioned oats

2 tablespoons tahini

2 tablespoons sesame seeds, ground

4 tablespoons raisins, chopped

1 teaspoon freshly squeezed lemon juice

a pinch of salt

ground cinnamon, to taste

container (about 9 x 6 in./24 x 15 cm), lined with plastic wrap (cling film)

Makes about 16 bars

Mash the bananas, then add all the remaining ingredients and mix well.

Put the mixture into the prepared container and flatten with a silicone spatula until about ¼ in. (½ cm) thick. Cover and freeze for 30 minutes. This will not freeze the bars, only make them more solid.

Remove the bars from the freezer and cut into about 16 slices. If you are not going to eat them immediately, wrap them individually and store in the refrigerator. They will keep for about a week.

POWER UP YOUR BRAIN
Tahini is a paste made from ground sesame seeds. It is versatile as a part of a snack, salad dressing, or a yummy snack bar. Sesame seeds provide a whole food source of many vitamins and minerals, including manganese, copper, iron, calcium, essential fatty acids, vitamin E, and B-vitamins. All are protective for our brain as they contribute to stable moods, quick thinking, and executive function. Rich in fiber, sesame seeds can assist as a bowel-movement stimulant for some. Look for tahini made from unhulled sesame seeds for maximum nutritional value.

½ cup (90 g) dried dates, stoned (pitted)

½ cup (65 g) cashews

1 large teaspoon coconut oil

1½–2 teaspoons spirulina powder

1 large teaspoon matcha powder (green tea powder)

about ¼ cup (20 g) unsweetened dried shredded (desiccated) coconut

Makes about 16

Soak the dates in a bowl of water for 30 minutes, but no longer than that.

Put the cashews in a food processor fitted with an "S" blade and pulse for 30–45 seconds, until a thick meal has formed.

Rinse the dates, wipe off any extra moisture, and add them to the food processor along with the coconut oil, spirulina, and matcha powder. Process until a large ball starts to form. Remove the blade and take the processor bowl off the stand.

Using a small cup half-filled with water to wet your hands as you go, pinch off pieces of the mixture about the size of whole walnuts. Roll them into balls between the palms of your hands. (Damp hands will stop the mixture from sticking too much.)

Roll each ball in the coconut to coat it evenly, then place on a plate or board. Repeat with the rest of the mixture.

Refrigerate the energy bites for at least 20 minutes before eating. They will keep in an airtight container in the refrigerator for up to 3 weeks.

Spirulina and Matcha Brain-fitness Bites

A winning combination! Spirulina and matcha are brainpower foods filled with a major detox agent: chlorophyll, which binds toxins. Every single bite is filled with protein and potent health-supporting phytonutrients. Spirulina upregulates cognitive function and improves memory, while matcha, which contains caffeine, improves mental alertness and clarity and lowers stress.

PART 3

FOOD DIARY

Why Should You Keep a Food Diary?

Keeping a food journal is a great way to gain more clarity on which foods make us feel well and which ones make us feel tired and bloated. When you eat, you eat for the microbes in your gut. It sounds strange, but it is true. Are you eating foods that will help the diversity and balance of the microbiome, which directly affect your energy, mood, and ability to make empowered and rational decisions? Or are you consuming foods that give you a sugar rush, followed by a brain slump, and make you vulnerable to anxiety, a fuzzy mind, or depressed moods? Specific tracking of what we eat for a week reveals dietary habits that we might not be conscious of—and it is these that keep us from reaching our individual goals. A food diary makes one aware of how one might gravitate toward sugary or starchy foods or alcohol when one is emotionally upset, or how one can use caffeine as a picker-upper throughout the day. In addition, the dietary journal can help make sure that we get enough hydration, protein, and healthy fats in the daily diet.

A food diary is useful in discerning how, what, and when we eat directly affects our mood, sleep, energy, and overall wellbeing. Possible food sensitivities with digestive troubles, funky moods, fatigue soon after eating, food cravings, headaches after meals, and other symptoms can also be tracked.

Last, but not least, a food journal is an easy and effective way to keep us accountable every day for what goes into our mouth. If we have to write down "cheat foods," we may think twice before indulging and consider if we really are emotionally hungry, or truly need more food in our tummy. A food journal keeps us honest and raises our awareness.

You can choose to write as you go or set time aside to journal before going to sleep. You may wish to photocopy the food diary template on page 153 into a small notebook or use it as a template for a document on your computer. You could also use an app (there are many available).

How do you keep a food diary?

Each day, list and describe all of the food you eat at each meal and snack:

- Be specific about how it is cooked: raw, baked, fried, grilled etc.
- Make sure you include any extras, such as salad dressing, gravy, butter, sugar, or ketchup.
- List what you drink, too. Note how much water and any additional beverages that you drink in fluid ounces (milliliters).
- Make a note of when you eat each meal and snack.
- Include the amounts of each food or drink for each day—for example, a serving of 3 oz. (85 g) cooked protein is the size of a deck of cards, or count the amount of chips (crisps) you eat. For vegetables or fruits, record them in their raw or uncooked state, e.g. ½ cup of berries.
- Say where you eat each meal and snack and who you are with. Our eating environment matters, so write down if you are at home, in a car, or at work. Note whether you are sitting at a table in the dining room or in the kitchen, or standing at a counter. Are you with friends or family, or alone in a calm space? When dining out, write down the name of the restaurant or bar. All details matter in the big picture.
- Describe what you are doing while eating. Are you checking emails, watching TV, on the phone, or reading? All will affect your ability to digest well.
- It is important to write down how you feel when you eat. Are you stressed, bored, or upset? Or do you feel you are in a calm place and look forward to the meal ahead? A food diary is great for showing how we can develop non-serving eating habits if we are "emotionally hungry."
- Similarly, assess and note down your energy levels and also any health symptoms, such as digestive discomfort or any headaches.

Keep a note of portion size when writing your food diary—berries can be counted individually or measured in cups.

Helpful extras

- Note the time you get up and the time you go to bed. How and when you you go to sleep matters greatly. Sleep is the anti-aging factor and our brain needs sleep so it can get rid of toxins. By tracking when you go to sleep, you become aware of how your nutrition, caffeine, and alcohol consumption or exposure to technological devices can affect your ability to fall asleep and to stay asleep. It can also affect frequent urination and blood-sugar balance during the night. A low blood-sugar episode during the night will wake us up, as will a snoring partner. All affect the restorative action we need during sleep, and when you wake, you still feel tired. (Viral infections must have been ruled out as a possible cause.) Not sleeping well can make you feel tired, depressed, and cranky in the morning, inducing more carb cravings and the potential for headaches, poor concentration at work, and weight gain in the long term. Alternatively, perhaps you feel wired and are staying up too late so need to adjust your lifestyle?

Write down if you feel refreshed in the morning or struggle to wake up. Tracking in a journal is very revealing about why you might be tired despite getting eight hours of sleep.

- Note any exercise you participate in each day. Note the type of exercise and how long you do it for. Similarly, list any periods of relaxation and what they involved. Do you have enough quiet time to balance a busy lifestyle?

The golden rule is that you honor your commitment to yourself, and stay honest as you write in your diary every day. Do not rely on your memory to recall what you ate, drank, or thought yesterday. Food journaling is not to be considered a judgement of "being bad"

when one chooses to consume a food or drink that we know is not good for us. Consider the food and lifestyle diary as an exploration or observation of how you make better and preventative choices in life so that you can enjoy a fulfilling life with optimal cognitive function and good memory recall. We need a healthy brain, and we only have one. On a personal note, I prefer this perspective—what can I add into my life that builds health? Perfection is not the goal; the purpose of this diary is to make us mindful in making better choices more often. It makes us aware and teaches us to take responsibility for our choices—and we get to enjoy the reward.

Keep this food diary for seven days (unless you are dealing with medical considerations, undesired weight loss, or ongoing digestive troubles while under the care of a health professional, in which case ask them or your doctor for advice). You can always keep journaling if you find that it keeps you on a better track and enjoy the accountability aspect. However, after seven days you will have a much better idea of where you can increase diversity of foods, whether you need to drink more water during the day, or whether it is time to change your habits of eating oatmeal and banana every morning. Consider the diary as a self-awareness exercise and make small changes in your food planning, shopping list, and menu choices. See if you could benefit from drinking less alcohol or coffee, increasing the amount you walk every day, or going to sleep sooner. Choose an area that resonates most with you today to make a change that will impact your energy, mood, focus, and memory on a daily basis.

By keeping a food diary, you will gradually encourage yourself to make better and more varied food choices. Oatmeal and berries is a great breakfast but not when eaten every day!

Food Diary Template DAY _

WAKE UP: _____

MORNING MEAL   Time: _____
Food eaten: _____
_____

Where/activities/who you were with: _____

Mood/energy/health symptoms: _____
_____

SNACK   Time: _____

LUNCH   Time: _____
Food eaten: _____
_____

Where/activities/who you were with: _____

Mood/energy/health symptoms: _____
_____

SNACK   Time: _____

EVENING MEAL   Time: _____
Food eaten: _____
_____

Where/activities/who you were with: _____

Mood/energy/health symptoms: _____
_____

SNACK   Time: _____

How much water drunk: _____

Other drinks: _____

Any exercise or relaxation? _____

TIME TO BED: _____

USEFUL RESOURCES

WEBSITES

Environmental Toxicity

American Academy of Environmental Medicine
www.aaemonline.org

National Drinking Water Database
www.ewg.org/tapwater

www.ewg.org/release/new-guide-warns-dirty-dozen-food-additives

www.ewg.org/enviroblog/2016/07/today-s-secret-ingredient-traces-toxic-plastic-chemicals

Women's Voices for the Earth
www.womensvoices.org

www.safecosmetics.org

http://cdn.ewg.org/sites/default/files/EWGCellphoneTips.pdf

www.ewg.org/research/dirty-dozen-list-endocrine-disruptors

www.greenmedinfo.com/gmi-blogs-popular

www.westonaprice.org/environmental-toxins

Neurological Disease

www.alzheimerborreliosis.net

www.blaylockreport.com

www.drtenpenny.com

www.doctor-natasha.com/gaps-book.php

www.worldmercuryproject.org

Mold and biotixin illness:

www.survivingmold.com

Lyme Disease and Co-infections

www.ilads.org

www.klinghardtacademy.com

www.cangetbetter.com

Nutritional Resources

www.celiac.com

www.siboinfo.com

www.livestrong.com

www.mercola.com

www.thelowhistaminechef.com

www.gapsdiet.com

www.paleoleap.com

www.wellnessmama.com

www.bulletproofexec.com/61-gluten-sensitivity-celiacs-bulletproofing-your-gut-with-dr-tom-obryan-podcast

www.whole30.com/whole30-program-rules

www.thepaleomom.com/start-here/the-autoimmune-protocol

www.holistichelp.net/blog/sibo-treatment-diet-and-maintenance

www.sibodietrecipes.com

www.breakingtheviciouscycle.info

www.ediblenutmegmagazine.com/about

www.westonaprice.org/health-topics/vegetarianism-and-plant-foods

www.westonaprice.org/health-topics/cod-liver-oil-topics

www.marksdailyapple.com

Dentistry

www.westonaprice.org/dentistry

Health food options:

www.localharvest.org/spring-valley-ny

www.grasslandbeef.com

www.localharvest.org/new-york-ny

www.ohsheglows.com/2013/01/24/my-favourite-homemade-almond-milk-step-by-step-photos

Find Real Food Locations—Mobile App
www.findrealfoodapp.com

www.ewg.org/research/ewgs-good-seafood-guide/executive-summary

Wise Choice Market
www.wisechoicemarket.com

www.ewg.org/foodnews

Great Lakes Gelatin
www.greatlakesgelatin.com

Heritage Foods
www.heritagefoodsusa.com

Pure Indian Foods
www.pureindianfoods.com

Community Supported Agriculture (CSA)—Just Food
www.justfood.org/csa

Hawthorn Valley Farm
www.hawthornevalleyfarm.org

FURTHER READING

Nourishing Traditions: The Cookbook that Challenges Politically Correct Nutrition and Diet Dictocrats by Sally Fallon and Mary G. Enig

Breaking the Vicious Cycle: Intestinal Health Through Diet by Elaine Gloria Gottschall

Know Your Fats: The Complete Primer for Understanding the Nutrition of Fats, Oils and Cholesterol by Dr. Mary G. Enig

The Fourfold Path To Healing: Working With The Laws Of Nutrition, Therapeutics, Movement, and Meditation in the Art of Medicine by Dr. Thomas S. Cowan with Sally Fallon and Jaimen McMillan

Nourishing Traditions Book of Baby & Child Care by Sally Fallon and Thomas S. Cowan, MD

The Gut and Psychology Syndrome by Dr. Natasha Cambell-McBride

The Metabolic Typing Diet: Customize Your Diet To: Free Yourself from Food Cravings: Achieve Your Ideal Weight; Enjoy High Energy and Robust Health; Prevent and Reverse Disease by William L. Wolcott and Trish Fahey

A Clinical Guide to Blending Liquid Herbs by Kerry Bone MCPP FNHAA FNIMH DipPhyto Bsc (Hons)

Wild Fermentation and The Art of Fermentation by Sandor Katz

Feelings Buried Alive Never Die by Karol K. Truman

Daring Greatly: How the Courage to Be Vulnerable Transforms the Way We Live, Love, Parent, and Lead by Brene Brown

Nourish, Thrive, Heal: A Comprehensive and Holistic Approach to Living with Lyme Disease by Rika K. Keck

REFERENCES

PART 1

The Brain: Powering Your Day

"Anatomy of the Brain," Mayfield Clinic, www.mayfieldclinic.com/PDF/PE-AnatBrain.pdf

Christine B. Dalton and Douglas A. Drossman, "The Use of Antidepressants in the Treatment of Irritable Bowel Syndrome and Other Functional GI Disorders," UNC Center for Functional GI & Motility Disorders, www.med.unc.edu/ibs/files/educational-gi-handouts/IBS%20and%20Antidepressants.pdf

Melissa Lind, "List of Foods with Flavonoids," December 18, 2013, www.livestrong.com/article/73159-list-foods-flavonoids

"Microbes Help Produce Seratonin in Gut," Caltech, April 9, 2015, www.caltech.edu/news/microbes-help-produce-serotonin-gut-46495

"Skull," *Wow*, www.wow.com/wiki/Human_skull

Ying Xu et al., "Curcumin Reverses the Effects of Chronic Stress on Behavior, the HPA Axis, BDNF Expression and Phosphorylation of CREB," *Brain Research*, vol. 1122, no. 1 (November 29, 2006), pp. 56–64, www.sciencedirect.com/science/article/pii/S0006899306027144

The Gut–Brain Connection

Dr. Datis Kharrazian, www.drknews.com

Josh Axe, "Bone Broth Benefits for Digestion, Arthritis and Cellulite," www.draxe.com/the-healing-power-of-bone-broth-for-digestion-arthritis-and-cellulite

Kelly Brogan, "From Gut to Brain: The Inflammation Connection," November 2013, www.kellybroganmd.com/from-gut-to-brain-the-inflammation-connection

Garry Davidson, "Man Boobs and the Estrogen to Testosterone Ratio," Chest Sculpting, December 30, 2016, www.chestsculpting.com/man-boobs-and-the-estrogen-testosterone-ratio

Osha Key, "12 Foods to Fight Inflammation," July 12, 2013, www.mindbodygreen.com/0-10260/12-foods-to-fight-inflammation.html

John Staughton, "Does Bacteria in the Gut Affect Mood and Behavior?," May 2016, www.scienceabc.com/humans/does-bacteria-in-the-gut-stomach-affect-mood-and-behavior.html

Jennifer Wolkin, "Meet Your Second Brain: The Gut," August 14, 2015, www.mindful.org/meet-your-second-brain-the-gut

Joy Yang, "The Human Microbiome Project: Extending the Definition of What Constitutes a Human," National Humane Genome Research Institute, July 16, 2012, www.genome.gov/27549400/the-human-microbiome-project-extending-the-definition-of-what-constitutes-a-human

Friend or Foe Food List

"Beware of this Health Fake: Healthy Cereal that Isn't," *Food Babe*, http://foodbabe.com/2015/02/24/healthy-cereal

"The Fish You Can Eat, the Fish You Should Definitely Avoid: An Update," *Body Ecology*, www.bodyecology.com/articles/the_fish_you_can_eat_and_should_avoid.php

Rika K. Keck, *Nourish, Heal, Thrive: A Comprehensive and Holistic Guide to Living with Lyme Disease*, River Grove Books, 2016

Sara Schwartz, "5 Worst Foods for Your Brain," American Grandparents' Association, www.grandparents.com/health-and-wellbeing/diet-and-nutrition/worst-foods-for-your-brain

Foods to Support Energy, Mood, and Focus

S. A. Farr et al., "Extra Virgin Olive Oil Improves Learning and Memory in SAMP8 Mice," *Journal of Alzheimer's Disease*, vol. 28, no. 1 (2012), pp. 81–92, www.ncbi.nlm.nih.gov/pubmed/21955812

G. Münch et al., "Advanced Glycation Endproducts in Ageing and Alzheimer's Disease," *Brain Research. Brain Research Reviews*, vol. 23, nos. 1–2 (February 1997), pp. 134–43, www.ncbi.nlm.nih.gov/pubmed/9063589

Peter Andrey Smith, "The Tantalizing Links between Gut Microbes and the Brain," *Nature*, 14 October 2015, www.nature.com/news/the-tantalizing-links-between-gut-microbes-and-the-brain-1.18557

"Shocking! The 'Tequila' Sweetener Agave Is Far Worse than High Fructose Corn Syrup," March 30, 2010, *Mercola*, http://articles.mercola.com/sites/articles/archive/2010/03/30/beware-of-the-agave-nectar-health-food.aspx

"What Is Malitol? What Is Sorbitol? Know Your Sugar Substitutes! Better Yet, Know What Your Are Putting into Your Body!," February 26, 2010, www.hubpages.com/health/What-is-Maltitol-What-is-Sorbitol-Know-Your-Sugar-Substitues-Better-Yet-Know-What-you-are-Putting-into-Your-Body

Rotate Your Plate

"Food and Chakra Pairing: Balancing and Healing Our Energy Centers through Food," *Parsnips & Pastries* blog, June 17, 2016, www.parsnipsandpastries.com/chakra-food-pairing-balancing-healing-energy-centers-food

Zain Saraswati Jamal, "Balance Your Chakras with Food," *Gaia*, April 13, 2013, www.gaia.com/article/balance-your-chakras-food

Andrew Weil, "Mushrooms for Good Health?," February 17, 2014, www.drweil.com/diet-nutrition/nutrition/mushrooms-for-good-health

PHOTOGRAPHY CREDITS

All images © Ryland Peters and Small/CICO Books.
Key: *a* = above, *b* = below, *l* = left, *r* = right

Heather Cameron: pp. 66, 69, 87, 146
Peter Cassidy: pp. 10*bl*, 21*ar*, 27*r*, 51
Nicki Dowey: p. 23*l*
Tara Fisher: pp. 7*br*, 8, 19, 23*r*, 42bl, 84, 101, 102, 104, 143, 147, 151
Winfried Heinze: pp. 9, 10*ar*, 34, 30
Richard Jung: p. 10*al*
Erin Kunkel: p. 20
William Lingwood: pp. 7*ar*, 75, 116, 130, 131
David Merewether: pp. 13, 18
Steve Painter: pp. 21*al*, 21b, 36, 78, 83, 91, 92, 98, 109, 110, 113
William Reavell: pp. 27*l*, 45, 46
Hervé Roncière: pp. 29, 76, 77
Toby Scott: pp. 2, 7*al*, 17, 53, 55, 67, 107, 117, 125, 136
Lucinda Symons: p. 10*br*
Debi Treloar: pp. 38, 152
Stuart West: p. 41
Kate Whitaker: pp. 1, 28, 33, 42*al*, 58, 59, 61, 81, 88, 94, 97, 115, 132, 133, 148
Clare Winfield: pp. 4, 7*bl*, 14, 42*ar*, 42*br*, 57, 62, 65, 71, 72, 89, 122, 129, 135, 139, 140, 149

RECIPE CREDITS

Miranda Ballard: pp. 86, 90, 110, 111
Ghillie Başan: pp. 93, 126, 127, 145
Jordan Bourke: pp. 85, 100, 103, 105, 142, 147
Jordan & Jessica Bourke: pp. 59, 60, 80, 96
Heather Cameron: pp. 66, 69, 87, 146
Mat Follas: p. 112
Nicola Graimes: pp. 132, 133
Dunja Gulin: pp. 52, 54, 58, 67, 88, 95, 106, 114, 117, 124, 137, 148
Anya Ladra: pp. 74, 116, 130, 131
Michael van Straten: pp. 68, 76, 77, 108
Milli Taylor: pp. 118, 120
Belinda Williams: pp. 51, 79, 82, 99, 109
Jenna Zoe: pp. 56, 63, 64, 70, 71, 89, 123, 128, 134, 138, 141, 149

INDEX

ACKNOWLEDGMENTS

I would like to extend my appreciation to the many teachers, holistic practitioners, and physicians who have shared with me their wisdom, education, and clinical experiences.

I wish to thank my husband, who has been extremely patient while I was writing two books, and who provides me with homegrown organic vegetables from his garden.

I would also like to thank Kristine, Carmel, and Cindy from CICO Books who gave me this wonderful opportunity to share my brain-nourishing perspective in this must-have cookbook.